Glimmerings
and Stammerings

TWILIGHT
RUMINATIONS

Charles C. Finn

PRAISES FOR GLIMMERINGS AND STAMMERINGS

All art should make us think and without being didactic, Charlie Finn invites us to do just that - to ponder deeply the world around us and the lives that interconnect with us whether they be two-legged, four-legged or winged; to see beauty in the humblest places. He prods us to join him in recognizing the disparate, the injustices and inconsistencies that threaten our fragile planet. He prompts us to question and respond. Here is an itinerary prepared by a gentle guide, his poems like stations along the way, to pause and reflect. It's a journey that can be begun at any page, at any place and undertaken at any pace. Savor the poems slowly. Let these words guide your contemplations and inspire your actions.

—Jenny Chapman: Animist, observer and enthusiast of the natural world and admirer of the written word.

With surprise appearances in his poems by hummingbirds, Dolly Parton, Gandhi, Van Gogh, Rumi, a fox and …you never know what. This poet's keen eye and alert ear reveal a feast of images from every season of the year. Another course of the feast has arrived in Charlie Finn's Glimmerings and Stammerings. Enjoy!

—Joyce Rouse, songwriter and recording artist Earth Mama, EarthMama.org.

Charlie Finn's poems reveal divine beauty, growth pangs and a cosmic encouragement in our daily walk on Earth. His frankness, humor and cheer have accompanied many a planetary pilgrim through the decades, reminding us that no creature walks here alone and all are growing up for a great purpose.

—Liza Field, mountain advocate and conservationist.

Glimmerings and Stammerings, Charlie Finn's newest volume of poetry, is aptly named. There are few stammerings, but many glimmers of light at the corner of one's eye. Only closer reflection and rumination will reveal what the light has to tell us. Reading Charlie's poetry is always an adventure. There will be surprises, references to literature shared, mention of journeys and anniversary dates and important events. Daily life will be linked to the infinite, the human spirit to the spirits of animals and trees, and shared experiences brought to life in few words. In this volume, as always, many poems touched me. The one that seems to encapsulate many is "I Have Spoken." In silence, in worship, in talking circles, in writing, and in being, Charlie has indeed spoken. And in so doing, he challenges all of us to do the same.

—Sue Williams, retired Quaker peacemaker and political mediator, whose publications include Being in the Middle by Being at the Edge.

My friend Charlie is a poet who spends time each day listening, watching and being. Then the words come and he writes them down so we too can see ordinary things in extraordinary ways. James Baldwin believed poets were the only people who knew the truth about us. This could be true, but what is certainly true is this: Charlie's poems help us unearth truths about ourselves, our environment and our God and as a result the world, our whole wonderful, messy, chaotic world is a little bit better for it.

—Joy Sylvester-Johnson, CEO Emeritus of the Roanoke Rescue Mission.

Poets are ruminants, magically transforming their daily grazings into metaphorical bone and sinew and flesh. Charlie Finn, the author of this generous collection of liminal gifts, once observed that, "It slows you down / to wake you up / to a corner of creation / waiting to astonish. / A poem." According to an old saying, an apple a day keeps the doctor away. For those slowing down enough to savor the poetry in this fine volume, it could equally be said that reading a poem a day helps keep the doldrums at bay.

—Robert Foote chops wood, hauls water, and tends the seasons in southwest Virginia.

Charlie's poems speak to me. They help me to remember how much magic there is all around me, with so much to see, and know, and feel. Wherever I am, whenever it is, and even when things seem a bit dark, there is magic to be found. These poems carry that message and I am always grateful.

—Joyce Foote, Quaker, human being, enamored of every living thing, most especially, at this point in her life, grandchildren!

Over the years I have come to savor each new volume of Charlie Finn's poetry. Each poem is a blooming flower, arresting with a sudden glimpse or opening slowly with words that build a story of love or an understanding of a universal truth. Our lives are richer for reading and hearing the unique verse and voice of Charlie Finn.

—Richard Rouse, author of The Welcome Home Door: Tales of Appalachia and Beyond (on Audible) and The Fairy Ring and Other Stories.

Living similar spirit journeys over a long lifetime, Charlie's ruminations, poems, speak to me, informing and inspiring. Surrounded by nature and making room for solitude give us entry into the great mystery. We realize that we are all connected, with contemplation leading us to actions of love and service. I'm looking forward to more of Charlie's ruminations in the morning light. Glimmerings and Stammerings, another gift book of blue plums, to nurture us and to enjoy at day's end.

—Herb Beskar, retired Social Worker still active supporting asylum-seekers living in the Roanoke region.

Charlie Finn's poetry stands at the threshold of who I am and who I might become.

—Robert Guthrie, a retired Roanoke psychotherapist who cherished his work with Veterans, who loves the in between.

Charlie Finn teaches us to dig deep into life to discover our love of and connection to the world around us.

—Helen Guthrie is a fellow traveler with deep Jungian roots.

Like cairns in the wilderness, Charlie's words point us toward hidden landscapes, offering startling vistas disguised with unexpected layers of meaning. Exploring these new dimensions with us, this modern mystic's visionary insight leads us down paths linking our heads and hearts in empathetic union with every vibrant, sacred wonder of creation he casts his poetic gaze upon. As he informs our imagination and helps awaken us to this newly discovered world, we are apt to revel in wide-eyed amazement and heart-felt insight with appreciation for a universe of unforeseen opportunities.

—Kent Walton, tree lover.

When I began this slim book of poetry, I thought that reading it would be an addition to my early morning meditations. I thought I would read a page or so a day, but found that reading the poems had a similar affect on me as the consumption of good potato chips: I could not stop with just one! The author's thoughts and observations did indeed enhance how I interpret the events of the day. I look more carefully, I pause more often.

—Sharon Custer-Boggess, Student of the Buddha, Mindfulness/Meditation Practitioner.

Glimmerings and Stammerings is *not* for snacking! Although it is filled with tiny bites, it is a full course meal! Prepare to be nourished as well as delighted!

—Susan Adams, lover of Palestine from rich years spent there.

How is it possible to describe for you the timeless and timely nature of Charlie Finn's poetry? From individual experiences to the collective ones, he encapsulates the full range of human qualities in life: joy, wonder, innocence, complexity, sorrow, grief, curiosity, humor, kindness, spirituality, and the list goes on. Imaginative and playful, prayerful and longing, he finds a way to invite us into an intimate world with universal application. His appreciation of the natural world and the integration of soul and spirit within it are compelling. His writing finds the still places within the storm. His breadth of knowledge, his depth of heart and his attentiveness bring his writing to life. These poems are thoughtful, provocative and original!

—Marian Barrett Leibold, Spiritual Director.

I have been inspired and changed by the poetry and prose of Charlie Finn since he began writing and, in recent decades, publishing. Glimmerings and Stammerings is a year-long passage through his life. Get ready for the mystic's eye capturing the moment and the ordinary. Get ready for the depth of expression into areas unknown. Enjoy the light …and feel the twilight and darkness capturing your own mysterious presence. Each poem informs an insight known by one man traveling through many years of crafting words to both arouse and soothe others on their own transcendent journey. Take time with each passage and savor the spirit that emerges.

> **—John M. Dougherty, Ph.D. Retired, Professor of Psychology in Psychiatry at the University of North Carolina – Chapel Hill School of Medicine.**

Charlie Finn is a practitioner of observation with open eyes, reflection with open mind, empathy with open heart, wordcraft with care and exuberance and love. Readers are invited to escape the noise and hurry, and spend some quiet time in these pages — poetic gifts from a fellow seeker-celebrant of the Divine in our everyday lives.

> **—Kevin O'Keefe, a Colorado transplant from Chicago enamored of mountains, music, grandchildren, and good poetry.**

Read at your peril! A warning for experiencing radical amazement! Charlie lovingly, but persistently, and always joyfully, encourages his readers to savor moment to moment the world around and within each of us. Whether one reads "Glimmerings and Stammerings" chronologically or serendipitously, the richness of the ever-changing kaleidoscope of his experiences will challenge the reader to live as fully as possible with more awareness, humility, and awe.

> **—Chris Dougherty, a novice mystic.**

Publisher's Cataloging-in-Publication Data

Names: Finn, Charles C. Finn, author.

Title: Glimmerings and Stammerings/Charles C. Finn
Identifiers: LCCN: 2024903416 | ISBN 979-8-9893575-4-3 (Paperback) |
979-8-9893575-5-0 (eBook)

BISAC POETRY / General | POETRY/ American / General

Cover and book design by Asya Blue Design

Front cover: An amaryllis shimmering in the radiant gold
of the rising sun — Photo by Charles C. Finn.

First Edition

Visit the author's website at https://poetrybycharlescfinn.com/

DEDICATED

⌒

to all spirit journeyers
and lovers of twilight

CONTENTS

AUTHOR'S FOREWORD

⌒

"Glimmerings" hints at light, spied askance from different angles. "Stammerings" announces futility—words, too, hint at best. Two passages from Frederick Buechner's *The Alphabet of Grace* will serve as an invitation to ponder words rising from a pilgrim spirit, enamored of twilight, across the rough span of a year, March 2022 to April 2023. The first invites writer and reader to recognize their affinity.

> "Who you are I do not know, and yet perhaps I know something. I know that like me you wake each morning to a day that you must somehow live, to a self that you must somehow be, and to a mystery that you cannot fathom if only the mystery of your own life. Thus, strangers though we are, at a certain level there is nothing about either of us that can be entirely irrelevant to the other. Think of these pages as *graffiti* maybe, and where I have scratched up in a public place my longings and loves, my grievances and indecencies, be reminded in private of your own. In that way, at least, we can hold a kind of converse. And there is always some comfort in knowing that Kilroy also was here." (*viii*)

The second touches directly on both glimmering and stammering.

> "We have seen more than we let on, even to ourselves.
> Through some moment of beauty or pain, some sudden
> turning of our lives, through some horror of the twelve
> o'clock news, some dream, some breakfast on the first
> and last of all our days, we catch glimmers at least of
> what the saints are blinded by. Only then, unlike the
> saints, more pigs always than heroes, we tend to go on
> as though nothing has happened. To go on as though
> something has happened even though we are not sure
> what it was or just where we are supposed to go with it,
> is to enter that dimension of life that religion is a word
> for…One thinks of Pascal sewing into his jacket, where
> after his death a servant found it, his 'since about half-
> past ten in the evening until about half-past midnight,
> FIRE. Certitude. Certitude. Feeling. Joy. Peace,'
> stammering it out like a child because he had to. Fire,
> fire, and then the scratch of pen to paper. There are
> always some who have to set it down in black and
> white." (76)

As for this book's subtitle, for as long as I can remember I've been drawn to liminal twilight times, none more than dawn and dusk. The changing of the guard. Or better, lovers softly whispering before reluctantly bidding adieu, until next time around. An octogenarian now (strange in my ears is that word still), I feel twilight's allure even more for having me claimed.

May the glimmerings and stammerings to follow, pilgrim reader, invite ruminations of your own, best remembered (if you're like me) in twilight.

INTRODUCTION

A s for the proper way to approach these ruminations from the twilight, there is none. While they are in chronological order, covering March of 2022 to April of 2023, there is no need to start at the beginning. A more spirited way of beginning a new relationship (books too can become friends) might be to cast your eyes over titles in Contents (there are quite a few) and start checking out some you find intriguing. You'll know soon enough if there are things here to feed you, draw you further in. I could only smile when a friend recently informed me he finally finished *Blue Plums on a Mat of Leaves*, my most recent volume of poetry, reading but one or two poems a day. Like wine, poetry is best savored.

A good novel is a page-turner, meant by the thrust of its story to carry the reader suspensefully forward. A good poem is a page-ponderer, station-stop instead of long-distance ride, aiming vertical instead of horizontal. Think of the poems to follow as ruminations hoping to spark in fellow spirit travelers their own ruminations, best pondered in twilight.

In Egypt I strongly identified with a statue of a scribe sitting at the feet of his Pharaoh behind him, papyrus and stylus ready, listening.

Ready for Whatever

Just when I feel nothing is coming—
pen idle in hand,
pad blank on lap—
eyes light on an object,
mind fastens on a memory,
imagination takes flight on a notion,
heart remembers an affection,
fear jumps up taunting,
"You're not done with me, buster,
I'll never stop haunting!"
Pen in hand and pad on lap,
scribe is ready for whatever. 4/20/22

Ponder elated
that the universe and you
aren't unrelated! 4/1/22

Bringing it closer home.

Empowered to Make a Difference

As foreboding as the times are,
allow that the fact that you're here
means you're carried by the energy of the universe,
empowered to make a difference. 4/1/22

Enter Vincent.

Canvasses Standing Ready, Vincent's and Yours

Vincent began each day with a blank canvas—
what wild dream in the night
or arresting scene before his sight
he could now forge into fiery existence!
When your head hits the pillow this evening
trust something will be emblazoned
on the canvas that stood blank in the morning
giving witness to your own wild dream in the night
or new event entering your sight
calling you to forge something new in the universe
into fiery existence! 4/1/22

Michelangelo shouts from the wings, Don't forget me!

When Your Feet Hit the Floor

Determine to free a David from the marble
when your feet in the morning hit the floor—
what else are you here for? 4/1/22

Thirty-two may seem excessive, but just imagine our joy to have that many.

> The whole winter long
> thirty-two amaryllis
> trumpeting beauty! 4/1/22

Is empathy even conceivable without imagination?

> imagination
> stretching from deep heart center
> becomes empathy. 4/2/22

Strange things cross your mind when another's eyes on you are fastened.

While Sitting with Eyes Closed

> Peeking to see my dog's eyes on me
> alert for sign of action
> calls to mind God. 4/2/22

Consciousness calls for courage.

Brace Yourself

> So much beauty,
> so much pain—
> if your goal is to keep your heart open
> brace yourself. 4/2/22

The age of nations, dreamed Teilhard, is past.

A Call to a Wider Patriotism

What could be more dangerous
than pledging allegiance
to nation-state over Earth? 4/2/22

I love when I'm stopped in my tracks.

Gratuities Keep Coming

What did I do
to deserve heron's blue flash
over the dark pond this morning?
Absolutely nothing. 4/3/22

*A query given by our Zoom instructor: What is your reaction to a
homeless person with a sign?*

Preying or Praying?

Were I dressed like a bum
with a plea on a placard,
would I more likely be a con man
preying on the gullible
or a humiliated one down and out
praying for a helping hand? 4/4/22

A reverie when gazing on our bloomless magnolia.

Wind Enough to Sing

I planted a magnolia years ago
too close to towering trees
making it impossible for it to blossom
for insufficiency of sun.
O but what clacking the wind makes
through those lustrous stiff leaves!
Until we find sufficient sun to flower
may we feel wind enough to sing. 4/3/22

"Rama, Rama, Rama"—his last words after being shot.

His Prayer was Answered

Gandhi long prayed
he would have forgiveness in his heart
and God on his lips
should he meet a violent death.
His prayer was answered. 4/5/22

Re-envisioning the Eden Story

A Decided Leap Forward

One could not be in God's image and likeness
if incapable of loving
and could not possibly have come to love
without knowledge of the fruit of the tree.
Hail Adam for taking the first bite,
Eve for cajoling him,
wise serpent in touch with Earth
for whispering in her ear.
Instead of the Fall
call it the Decided Leap Forward
toward the image and likeness! 4/6/22

Diehard sports fans need to step back.

Regaining Perspective

Diehard sports fans are deflated
when their bubble bursts
until they regain perspective.
Ukrainians are fleeing for their lives. 4/5/22

Pondering a gift from the East.

Om Mani Padme Hum

What better image than a jewel
to capture adamantine essence,
indestructible bedrock,
immortal diamond.
Mani.
What better image than a lotus,
blossom symbolizing beauty's ever-fleeting,
dying as soon as born,
evanescence in essence.
Padme.
The great mantra reminds us
we've not clashing foes here
for the jewel is *in* the lotus,
the immortal is *in* the mortal,
the kin-dom instead of at a far remove
is at hand! 4/6/22

See the difference a change of pronouns makes.

Unimaginable

Before saying to another,
"I'll never forgive you,"
imagine God saying that to you.
She wouldn't. 4/7/22

Imagine when you rise today what you might teach God. Blasphemy or revelation?

> Marvel to ponder
> that through you God keeps learning.
> No day is futile. 4/7/22

> Welcome with kindness
> the next person that you meet.
> How else save the world? 4/7/22

"Repent!" Where is the Baptist when we need him?

Repentance is the Tilling

> For seeds to be welcomed,
> soil winter-hardened must be tilled.
> Is it really any different
> when it's hearts that have hardened?
> Repentance is the tilling. 4/7/22

Supposedly God can't weep because beyond change, but then what's this about embodying love?

Hard to Imagine God Indifferent

Seeing how we disrespect
not only each other but Earth,
I find it hard to imagine
God being indifferent. 4/7/22

Before reacting to a frown with a frown, imagine what's behind it.

Next Frown You See

We say down in the mouth
but mean down in the heart.
Next frown you see,
beam out compassion. 4/7/22

How sad to fight back the tears.

Trust heart is speaking
when eyes begin to moisten.
Recognize the gift. 4/7/22

Audible gasps speak volumes.

Where there is Love there is Home

"Where there are friends there is country,
where there is love there is home."
An audible gasp was heard in the room
after these words from the Dalai Lama,
exiled from his native land in 1959
but finding everywhere home. 4/7/22

Stiff upper lip hides heart.

Allow Rivers to Carve Channels

With each new departure of a love,
our hearts will become wealthier
for the vast added treasure
but not before rivers are allowed
to carve channels down our cheeks. 4/8/22

A justification for saving old journals.

Words, too, Can Become Shrines

Forty years ago today
I left words on a page in my journal
capturing a burning moment that to reread
reignites the incandescence.
Words, too, can become shrines. 4/9/22

Something to ponder when one loved nears the end.

Love's Presence will not End

The journey of a friend
easing into the embrace of hospice
can be thought to be nearing an end
until it's remembered how far she'll yet travel
in long years to come
in the heart of each friend.
Love's presence does not end. 4/9/22

I look out windows,
see I'm surrounded by trees.
How lucky is that? 4/9/22

Listening to wise ones banter lifts the heart.

Even When They're Gone They'll Live On

Listening to two men cherished for their wisdom
banter on the necessity of joy
is balm for those weighed down with sorrow.
Even when they're long gone—
the Dalai Lama and Desmond Tutu—
the radiance from their joy will live on. 4/10/22

I find it fruitful to reread my old journal.

Moose Ready to Bellow

"Empowering realization—
I have something to give and *want* to!"
I hadn't yet given him a name,
but looking back on words written long ago
clearly ready to bellow was Moose! 4/11/22

The Titanic got me thinking.

Savor Each Day Still Afloat

A mountain of ice
looms ahead for us each—
there's no getting around it.
Savor each day still afloat. 4/11/22

Ah, the very word hummingbird sings.

Ruby-Throated Alleluia

Pity not a hummingbird mind
for not drinking deeply from a single chalice
(like ant in peony's velvet fold).
Imagine instead a ruby-throated alleluia
drinking in sips the entire garden! 4/12/22

Creativity has little room for self-pity.

The Face of One Offering an Ear

Had shame consumed him
it's doubtful Vincent would have done a portrait
of himself with head bandaged.
This simply is the face
of one offering an ear. 4/12/22

What price will we pay if he gets off scot-free?

Was the Boasting Guy Right?

May the Department of Justice
not shrink from pursuing it
fearing if The Don gets his just due
his rabble will take to streets.
Isn't it enough he's already escaped
under cover of Party cowering
conviction for two impeachments?
The guy boasting he could get away
with cold-blooded murder,
was he right? 4/12/22

Just imagining.

Sick with Fear and Sorrow

Wherever he had been laying his head
(Bethany is the best bet),
think of the dismay bordering on dread
when he didn't return that Thursday evening.
What a night they must have spent—
Mary and Martha, Magdalene too,
and then there was his mother—
all sick with fear and sorrow
at what they might learn tomorrow. 4/13/22

*You don't disturb the peace in an occupied land
without paying a price.*

Audacious Preacher Man

Imagine the glee of the soldiers
getting their hands on this upstart,
audacious preacher man
daring to disturb Pax Romana. 4/13/22

Thirteen years ago this day my breath was taken away.

Spirit Palpably Present

What I most remember when visiting the UN
was a darkened meditation room—
creation of Dag Hammarskjold—
off to the right upon entering
with beams of light angling down
onto an ancient black slab in the center.
Hushed time there will be remembered,
cannot be forgotten. 4/13/22

A Good Friday is nailed into America's memory.

The Single Consolation

The day is here again
when with the end of the bloody war imminent
the President and Mrs. Lincoln set out
for a relaxing evening at the theater.
That an earlier carriage ride had been joyful
is the single consolation. 4/14/22

Listen to Dolly and hear more than a country music star.

Radiating from Dolly Parton

Over the years I've taken the measure
of a true American treasure—
not just buoyant song but bright humanity
radiating from Dolly Parton. 4/14/22

I invite readers to remember when a steady gaze held them.

When a gaze holds you,
words are the last thing needed.
Each will remember. 4/14/22

A city is not unlike a person.

Memories of Extremes

Sometimes when in DC
I imagine the euphoria on a Friday
when word arrived from Appomattox,
and then an exact week later
on a Friday called Good
the horror upon hearing
about a bullet to a brain.
No different from the rest of us,
DC carries memories of extremes. 4/15/22

It's hard to block out war.

Where *are* They?

Worrying about my dog Buckley in the kennel
without his people for days
(where *are* they, where *are* they?)
gets me thinking about dogs in Ukraine
(where *are* they, where *are* they?).
Only one difference but a big one—
in just a few days
Buckley's people will return. 4/15/22

May from Olympian heights Keats be smiling.

It's Just an Old Urn

"Beauty is truth"—
such an airy platitude, what could it mean?
"Truth is beauty"—
come on now, John Keats,
quit mixing apples and oranges.
"That is all ye know on earth
and all ye need to know."
O these poets always messing with our minds.
Besides everybody can see
it's just an old urn. 4/22/22

From Keats to Hopkins.

He Also Read to Us Hopkins

The assistant to the Novice Master
used to teach us all manner of manners
from the right way to make a bed
or wait a table or even fold a letter.
"Think of **FeBRiLe**," he would say regarding the latter,
"front to back, right to left."
Who knew there was a right way to fold a letter?
Funny the things you remember sixty years back.
He also read to us poems of Hopkins
and ignited my soul. 4/22/22

Check out The Little Prince if you are wise.

Wisdom from a Fox

Something worth pondering
from a fox to a little prince.
"It is only with the heart
that one can see rightly."
Think of one unquestionably with heart
who sees you rightly.
Does it not fill you? 4/22/22

Things to consider when holding another in the Light. The quote is from The Inner Eye of Love by William Johnson.

Spooky Action at a Distance

"We can intercede for friends
by breathing the Spirit to them,
imagining that they are present
and that we are imposing hands on them."
These words stopped me in my tracks
with a new understanding of what it means
to hold another in the Light—
breathing Spirit to them,
laying hands across distance.
A phrase springs back from Einstein
begrudging the reality of the crazy quantum soup:
"spooky action at a distance"? 4/22/22

Separate and unconnected—are we really?

When Thinking of Presence

When thinking of presence
my mind flies to seven billion
breathing this instant.
Or is it a single Presence breathing us all,
animals, too, and don't forget trees? 4/23/22

Consider me blessed.

In the Company of Fire

Come April I bid woodstove farewell
and sunrise in stone circle hello.
Come October I bid sunrise farewell
and flaming in woodstove hello.
Either way I begin each day
in the company of fire. 4/25/22

His death poems are among D. H. Lawrence's finest.

When Drifting toward the Edge

How heartening to learn from his wife
that John Yungblut's favorite poem
as he was drifting toward the edge
was "Shadows" by D. H. Lawrence,
written when Lawrence himself
was drifting toward the edge.
"And if tonight my soul may find her peace
in sleep, and sink into good oblivion,
and in the morning wake like a new-opened flower
then I have been dipped again in God,
and new created."
Can you think of a brighter disposition
when drifting toward the edge? 4/27/22

Threat or opportunity? Expectation is the key.

Remember the Botanist's Pleasure

When preparing to meet a stranger
and inclined to feel dread,
remember the botanist's pleasure
on the brink of finding a new species.
Anticipate discovery instead. 4/25/22

Empathy might seem soft, but just try it.

Stiff Price Exacted by Empathy

We take umbrage when hearing
"It's not all about you"
for striking so true.
The stiff price empathy exacts
is letting go of self-absorption,
caring enough to imagine what's going on
in the heart of another. 4/27/22

Sometimes a book shakes the ground you stand on.

More Wisdom than You Can Wave a Wand At

There's more wisdom than you can wave a wand at
in Stephen Cope's *The Great Work of Your Life*.
Dharma, for starters, takes on new meaning
and the Bhagavad Gita on dusty shelves
leaps into surprising significance.
Woven throughout are figures well known—
Frost, Thoreau, Tubman, Keats, Whitman, Gandhi,
Beethoven and Susan B. Anthony among them—
each living out their dharma.
Come be dazzled by a new perspective
on the great work of your life. 4/28/22

Did you ever wonder how the fox came by his wisdom?

Someone Must Have Tamed You

From the fox to the Little Prince:
"It is only with the heart
that one can see rightly.
What is essential is invisible to the eye."
Such wisdom, little fox.
Someone must have tamed you
else how would you know? 4/29/22

What we say at the beginning of the day goes a long way.

What Will I Bring the Morning?

There's a world of difference
between what will the morning bring
and what will I bring the morning. 4/29/22

Each month sings a different song.

May Day Prayer

Beltane,
glory of mid-spring,
Mary's month beginning.
May this May day start
delight and embolden every heart! 5/1/22

Revolutionary is the concept of a free press. Authoritarians must root it out.

Straight from the Fascist Playbook

The weaker the fourth estate
the weaker the democratic state.
Straight from the fascist playbook:
"Down with the enemy of the people!" 5/1/22

It breaks your heart sometimes to watch the news.

O Mariupol

I can't for the life of me
get Ukraine out of my mind.
It's one thing to know
there's always somewhere war,
but to see the footage every night on the news!
O Mariupol,
desperate parents fleeing with terrified children
from the wreckage of their homes—
humans, how could you?
Peacemakers come. 5/2/22

If ecclesia means blessed assembly, shouldn't that include trees and birds?

Incense in Church

Part of my morning ritual
in a stone circle in the woods
is lighting a stick of incense.
After all, is this not church? 5/3/22

Since it could have been anywhere, the whole woods is holy.

For Dromia I Have the Entire Woods

My beloved cat Dromia
twenty-six years ago today
just like that disappeared.
Aging but not ailing,
something in the woods likely got him.
For other members of my animal family
I have the holiness of a burial place
where I smile to feel their presence.
For Dromia I have the entire woods. 5/3/22

When you grow up loving baseball, metaphors are abundant.

A Poetry/Baseball Connection

The instructor's quiet pronouncement
that my poem was flawless
has stayed with me down the years,
perhaps not unlike a batter letting slide into oblivion
countless swings missing the mark
but never an unforgettable moment
when knocking it out of the park. 5/4/22

*I remember the song growing up, never fathoming the
profundity of the wish.*

Vaya con Dios

May it flood her heart
to hear "Vaya con Dios"
as she readies for departure,
reminded she has company for the flight. 5/4/22

A new slant on Jesus and William Blake.

Blake Searched High and Low

That Blake searched ancients high and low
to identify what most marked Jesus
and fastened upon forgiveness
tells you something illuminating
about both Jesus and William Blake. 5/4/22

Ruminating on fog in the woods.

Metaphors Enrich

When fog settles in I smile to remember
both the cloud of unknowing
and Eliot's little cat feet.
Metaphors enrich. 5/4/22

The next two relate to pondering my hands on a flight to Seattle.

Cover to cover
(no book close at hand to read)
I'm reading my hands. 5/5/22

Stories behind the Misshapen

To look at their hands you could pity the aging—
skin mottled by sun,
knuckles misshapen,
fingers angling akimbo,
joints stiffened with aching—
until you watch their eyes
as you listen to them telling
whose skin they caressed,
fur they fluffed,
trowel they fondled,
bark they felt,
maul handle they gripped,
pen they plied
with what can only be called affection.
If we but knew the stories
behind the misshapen. 5/5/22

Graphic depiction of humanity's extremes

Anniston, May 1961

Who's to be most pitied—
those risking all for a cause
dragged from torched bus and beaten
or those with a cause of their own
torching, dragging, and beating?
Humanity at its best and worst here,
only one group deserving pity. 5/4/22

Tolkien left a mark.

Mentors Disguised as Wizards

Mentors come in all sizes,
in countless disguises.
How many times,
content like Bilbo anticipating tea at 4,
has there come the rude rapping
of a Gandalf at our door?
Go away! We protest stoutly
clinging to convenience.
"Make haste," he ignores,
"your gifts are needed!"
May we smile years hence as did Bilbo
to have found the courage not to ignore
mentors disguised as wizards
rudely rapping on our door. 5/6/22

A gem from J. D. F. Kitto's The Greeks, treasured across decades.

Pondering Arête

The closest we can come to the meaning of arête—
the Greek ideal in every endeavor—
is excellence.
What would it mean if we strove to excel
in literally everything we do,
not strive for an abstract perfection
but simply draw mind/body/spirit
into the task at hand? 5/17/22

Futile effort to capture the uncapturable—that glorious first Alaska morning!

Great Day in the Alaska Morning

Astounding first morning—
top deck at dawn,
encircling snow-capped mountains,
boat thrumming forward,
in the far distance tiny puffs
rising then falling—
could it be, it *had* to be,
spume from approaching humpbacks!
Great day in the Alaska morning! 5/17/22

Seeing glaciers up close, I'm reminded of justice.

On Glaciers and Justice

Two glaciers up close—
Margerie within thrilling earshot
of icebergs thunder birthing,
then up to the edge of Mendenhall
awed by the splendor of the slow massive flow.
Theodore Parker spoke of justice
towards which the moral arc bends.
Henceforward justice will call to my mind
El Capitan waiting to be sculpted
by the wonder and the splendor
of compassion's slow massive flow. 5/17/22

Alaska called back William Clark's heart cry long ago.

O the Joy

"O the joy!"
That was all William Clark could write in his journal
upon seeing the Pacific Ocean!
And here we are centuries beyond
with the same gigantic heart response.
Eagles, orcas, humpbacks, glaciers—
O the joy!
Towering Sitka spruce, western hemlock,
and red cedar carved into Eagle and Raven
witnessing ancients enduring—
O the joy!
All hands on deck each with a story
servicing our every need—
youth announcing hope for the world
with the audacity of their polar plunge!
O the joy!
Seasoned guides charting for us a course
in the footsteps of John Muir
opening our minds to new knowledge,
eyes to new wonders,
souls to new reverence for the Earth temple.
O the joy!
Fellow voyagers,
strangers but a week prior but strangers no longer,
bonded now not only by the glory of Alaska
but by friendship!
O the joy! 5/11/22

CHARLES C. FINN

Social situations often spark an exchange between Mouse and Moose.

Trading Chitchat for Genuine

Never good at chitchat
Mouse was decidedly anxious at the prospect
of sitting at meals with complete strangers,
but Moose decided early to trade chitchat for genuine.
Voila, by each meal's end on a cruise ship in Alaska
there were fewer complete strangers. 5/17/22

No wonder the mother of the Muses was Memory.

Memory's Kaleidoscope

Were it not for my wife
I'd have been content to sit in my tree cathedral
dreaming of Alaska.
But thanks to the thrust of her propulsion
wonders now keep bursting into view
to return years hence with each twist
of memory's kaleidoscope. 5/19/22

How to nail Revelation down if Creation is unfinished?

Why Dwell in a Land of Anti-Climax?

I hear bells and whistles
whenever pondering ongoing revelation.
Why dwell in a land of anti-climax
where all's been said and done
if when the work of Creation
emphatically is *not* done?
If it's important to find it in Scripture,
check out John quoting Jesus
saying thanks to Spirit's inbreaking
greater things are to come! 5/18/22

No longer constrained by doctrine, my imagination wheels free.

What Love-Mischief Today?

Just imagine that the Universe Spirit—
called by a thousand names including Daddy by Jesus
or no name by those satisfied with Mystery—
knows no better than we
what by day's end each will have fashioned,
loves no less than we to be surprised.
Hafiz caught it perfectly:
"There are two of us housed in this body.
What love-mischief, God,
can we do for the world today?" 5/18/22

Alaska is far more than the scenery.

Standing Higher than a Totem

On the Alaskan island of Kake
four native encounters are etched forever.
Young man returning from college to stay,
thrilling the hearts of his elders.
Woman donning proud regalia
to tell of the ways of her people.
Craftsman demonstrating with three adzes
how he carves a ceremonial mask.
Korean War veteran almost ninety
proudly telling a tale intricately carved
onto a 137-foot-high totem.
Higher than said totem Kake's humanity
stands in my memories of Alaska. 5/19/22

Early morning rejoicing to hear a call answered.

Our Fondest Hope

There were identical birdsongs this morning,
one close, one in the distance answering—
most heartening was the answering.
Isn't that our fondest hope—
our presence in the world acknowledged,
our call answered? 5/20/22

Can there be too many poems about friendship?

> Friends: never alone—
> purest gold securely tucked
> in the heart pocket. 5/18/22

When referring to a dream, David Whyte once spoke of "a cargo of revelation." It's been many years, but I haven't forgotten.

Cargo of Revelation

> The royal road to the Unconscious—
> Jung's words come back about dreams
> as I ponder last night's cargo of revelation. *5/20/22*

> When things become dire
> we can throw in the towel
> or call back our fire. *5/22/22*

While mulling on cosmogenesis....

Trust in the Not-Yet

> Not only does an electric current
> course through the ten thousand things
> but its thrust is upward on the wings
> of trust in the Not-Yet. 5/23/22

The heart loves to remember.

Remembering My Daughter's First Recital

This morning's dawn breaking
calls back Morning Has Broken
played by my daughter's eight-year-old fingers
in her very first recital
twenty-nine years ago today.
As if that weren't heart-brimming enough,
her next piece wonderfully wrought,
beautifully caught,
was Ode to Joy!
I have to believe
that along with her parents in the hall
Beethoven's heart too brimmed over,
ready to explode upon hearing his ode
brought to life once again
this time by eight-year-old fingers. 5/23/22

When a new name is given, it becomes lodged in your being.

Tree Listener

Staying awake through the dark,
encircled by white pines and prayer flags,
listening to a thousand night sounds,
I reviewed my life and cried for a vision.
After leaning in to hear what transpired,
my guide later bestowed on me a name
I'll always hold sacred.
How better to sanctify an experience
than having a name to mark it? 5/23/22

But the tip-top of a mountain of meaning.

The Lode Star of Mother

I was named for my mother's father
and for a middle name bear her own
grounding me perhaps for my journey
questing the lode star of Mother. 5/23/22

Don't just throw out quotes—
share how they've opened your heart,
touched the core of you. 5/23/22

Agnosticism has a bad press. Really now, is there one who knows absolutely what comes next?

Not Knowing Opens Wonder

"When it's over it's over,
and we don't know, not any of us,
what happens then
so I try not to miss anything…"
Thanks for the reminder, Mary Oliver,
that not-knowing needn't strike dread,
can evoke wonder instead. 5/23/22

Spinning off from a common phrase.

If We Did Away with Death

"If I ran the world"—
an evocative snippet overheard
leading usually to the declaration
we'd be better off without death.
Just think for a clear-eyed moment
about life with no death.
Bet you can't.
So do we chuck the whole business
or recognize with astonishment
that presumed opposites are really partners
in the wild cosmic Dance? 5/23/22

A gesture to start the day right.

Rooted and Reaching

I put my arms each morning
around a hickory next to my stone circle—
stand-in for all trees,
for all my relations.
This helps root me during the day
as I reach for the sun. 5/23/22

From a native's presentation on the Alaskan island of
Kake came a new image for dying.

Sometimes Analogies Leap

"Walking into the forest."
When she mentioned this phrase—
her people's manner of viewing one passing—
I rejoiced to receive yet another metaphor
for crossing the Rainbow Bridge.
It is said analogies always limp,
I find sometimes they leap. 5/23/22

Keeping death before us—pathology or wisdom?

By Keeping Death in Sight

How must it be I wonder
thinking of a friend in hospice
to know you're dying?
Deep down don't we all know,
and by keeping death in clear sight
don't we cherish life more
before we take flight? 5/23/22

Trying to keep open to miracles.

There I've Done it Again

While giving lip-service to the possibility
of the miracle of transformation,
I can't imagine a mobster politician
not taking mendacity to the grave.
No lightning bolt I conceive of
could bring him to the humility of contrition
crying out Lord have mercy.
There I've done it again,
given the last word to darkness,
dismissing even the possibility
of the miracle of transforming light
announced by Buddha and Jesus. 5/25/22

These next three conspire to send you back to Thornton Wilder's Our Town.

But Then Something Comes Piercing

As plays go it's a short one
so homespun from a bygone day
(what's with the total lack of flair?)
and so slow-moving that by the end of Act Two
the audience then (or reader now)
might well be tempted to bail
(where's the plot, where's the action?).
But then something comes piercing in Act Three
so elemental that it stuns one into seeing.
If this prompts you to pick up *Our Town,*
my hope is you don't rush to Act Three.
The slow-moving, homespun lack of flair
has brilliantly set the stage spare
for an elemental piercing. 5/25/22

Slow Tempo till Act Three

Thornton Wilder on the slow tempo
preceding Act Three in *Our Town:*
"It is an attempt to find a value above all price
for the smallest events in our daily life."
It also set the stage
for the whammy to follow. 5/25/22

It's Never Too Late, WAKE UP!

Act Three of *Our Town*—
what imaginative leap!
Transported suddenly to the other side of death
(despite counsel against it for being too painful)
Emily has to go back to shout what she sees
but no one can hear her!
How not be struck by Wilder's stroke of genius?
From audience bored almost to tears
to audience shocked past tears to sobbing!
I imagine him smiling
(every creator on Earth smiling)
to have left something behind
shouting to sisters and brothers sleeping,
"It's never too late, WAKE UP!" 5/28/22

An exquisite May pleasure.

Bulging toward White Explosion

Buds incrementally bulging
toward white explosion
of beauty and fragrance in June—
magnolia promise in May. 5/26/22

What to do when stewing in one's juices, that is the question.

When Inwardly Churning

It's hard to discern when inwardly churning
(stewing in one's juices as they say)
whether to chase it out with a practical shout,
"Enough is enough, it's getting me nowhere!"
or to stay in one's seat but lower the heat
by pondering from a wider view
what purpose it might be serving,
all this churning unnerving? 5/26/22

Multiple decades it's taken to inch toward these next ones.

Be careful of Should,
tyrant ready to jail you
then throw key away. 5/27/22

Do less and not more
in order that you do well
what you're here to do. 5/27/22

Please, America, don't turn away.

Like Candles Snuffed Out

As hard as it was
to see every Friday on PBS
faces lost tragically to COVID,
tonight it got harder
when nineteen faces flashed on the screen
all aged around ten
plus two stalwart teachers
all like candles in a savage gust snuffed out.
Don't turn away from the horror, America.
Instead for the sake of your children
DO SOMETHING ABOUT YOUR
    GUN-ADDICTION. 5/28/22

Once Again Congress Sends Prayers

New normal:
yet another massacre,
once again Congress sends prayers. 5/28/22

Clinton we might forget, but not Maya at his inaugural.

Remembering Maya's Words of Hope

No better way to sing of Maya
on anniversary number eight of her flight from her cage
than to remember her words of hope:
"History, despite its wrenching pain,
Cannot be unlived, and if faced
With courage, need not be lived again." 5/28/22

Democracy is up against it.

Armed and White

No worry if "they" are in the majority
when patriots such as we are armed to the teeth
with the color of our skin and the Second Amendment!
5/30/22

We Must Stifle the Vote!

"For the sake of our future
we must stifle the vote
to stand with our forefathers
who never dreamed that they
someday would outnumber us!" 5/30/22

Words serve by helping us to remember.

At the Edge of a Pond Long Ago

Sitting at the edge of our pond
one evening long ago,
I had just cracked the bullfrog code
when suddenly brought out of my reverie
by my cat leaping to the comfort
of the niche behind my head.
Back and forth went croaking now understood—
"Now" "Wow!" "Now" "Wow!" "Now" "Wow!"-
as Dromia and I settled into tender contentment
at the edge of a pond long ago. 6/1 22

Of course we can't know, but wouldn't this be the best clue?

Foreshadowing the Beatific Vision

Wouldn't looking straight into eyes
dancing to see you,
flashing a heart's full embrace,
be the very best preparation
for meeting God face to face? 6/2/22

If you had to choose...

> Would not worse by far
> than one who has been betrayed
> be one betraying? 6/2/22

From John Keats: "I believe in nothing more than the holiness of the heart's affections and the truth of the imagination."

Affections of the Heart

> That I remember my first dog's birthday
> seventy-four years ago today
> tells you something both important and holy
> about affections of the heart.
> They go deep, last long
> (just possibly forever). 6/2/22

"Global warming" and "climate change" understate grossly. How about EARTH IN CRISIS?

House Burning

> When would be a good time
> were it *your* house burning
> to sound the alarm?
> How about Earth? 6/2/22

"Hate crime" an exaggeration? Hear the vitriol, see the fangs.

Are You Warped at Your Core, O America?

If chilling to me of light hue
hearing of the plot to spread terror
by discriminate murder,
then terrifying to those of darker hue
intended objects of said murder.
Are you warped at your core, O America,
unable to grow beyond this? 6/3/22

This is for capitalists presuming they're the good guys.

Where are the guard rails
to keep greedy ambition
from running rampant?

Where does justice fit
into capitalists' creed?
Trickle down, really? 6/3/22

No haiku but otherwise same theme.

Thinking of the Obscenely Rich

If the obscenely rich are deemed sick,
what of the system that spawned them?
If instead they are envied,
greed has become god. 6/3/22

All that's missing are the hoods, meaning it's safe now to be brazen.

"Jews will not replace us!
Blacks will not replace us!"
God save America. 6/3/22

Pondering the power of "I'm proud of you."

Look them in the eyes
while you slowly say the words—
they will remember. 6/3/22

*The context was preparing to co-lead a workshop on John Yungblut,
mystic and mentor. My interior dialogue was par for the course.*

Predictable Dance

⌒

Mouse:
It'll be a disaster,
a flop leaving folks shaking their heads
over a whole week wasted—
we're trying to cram too much in,
will run out of time,
cloud instead of clarify,
stammer instead of stun with revelation.
Moose:
Relax, it'll be great.
How can his vision not astound?—
Jung's individuation and Teilhard's cosmogenesis,
mysticism within common reach,
mentoring what it's all about.
We've done the preparation,
now trust Way will open. 6/4/22

⌒

Look through our history
and point to times if you can
when Black lives mattered. 6/4/22

54

Back in the 1960s and 1970s, many were opened to the riches of the East by the writings of Alan Watts.

Trickster Alan Watts

"A skin-encapsulated ego"—
Alan Watts loved nothing more
than to burst the balloon of our assumption
that this is all we are.
Some call him a sensual mystic,
I call him Trickster. 6/3/22

I wish I could be more sanguine

Listen for a Defense of the Indefensible

Enthusiasts for the Lie will be dissuaded
by no evidence to the contrary—
just wait and see.
When the January 6th Commission lays it out,
listen for a defense of the indefensible.
More likely they won't bother to watch,
minds locked tight as the skin
over their Patriot's drum. 6/5/22

You have to admit on the surface Quaker worship baffles.

Silent Worship

If nothing is happening
or so it appears
what in the world possesses these Friends
to keep coming back?
If you really want to know come see. 6/5/22

If ever a complex figure it was Teddy Roosevelt.

Balancing Teddy's Ledger

On the plus side of the ledger
were literally millions of acres
he set aside as a bulwark
against capitalistic encroachment.
King of conservation and preservation,
how not hail Teddy?
On the minus side what of his disdain
for millions of a different hue
whose land was brazenly stolen
on the pretext of eminent domain? 6/5/22

Einstein and Teilhard would seem archetypal adversaries when it comes to the universe, until you look closer.

Mystical Comes Closest

In Einstein's universe of changeless geometric laws,
to introduce Spirit into the equation
insults the perfection—
despite that, "Mystical comes closest."
In Teilhard's universe change is the constant,
Spirit's ever on the move.
One static, the other dynamic, but both emphatic
that mystical comes closest. 6/5/22

Where they starkly differ is where time fits in.

Einstein and Teilhard

Think space when you think Einstein—
the universe is!
Think time when you think Teilhard—
the universe is still becoming!
The gigantic difference breaks through
when the subject of the inquiry
shifts from the universe to you,
incontestably a child of the universe! 6/8/22

CHARLES C. FINN

Remembering a challenge met helps like nothing else when a new one pops up.

We've Navigated Troubled Waters Before

Stewing in my own juices,
floundering in choppy waters,
tossing and turning when sleep won't come—
until the waves calm,
it strikes me why not anchor it in a poem?
I trust there are other sailors
who understand floundering for having been there.
May we relax into calm remembering
that we've navigated troubled waters before. 6/6/22

If you cheered for it then but not now, what does that say?

Is It Really Less Dangerous?

In California back in the 60s
when Blacks armed themselves with assault weapons
Reagan saw to it as governor
that assault weapons were banned.
Is it really less dangerous
now that the skin hue is lighter
of those armed with assault weapons? 6/6/22

58

Meet one of the creatures in my mythology who, when I'm oppressively serious, helps lighten me up.

Goonyturds

Next time you recognize
you're weighed down with too serious—
the weight of it crushing—
imagine a flying squadron of goony birds
bombarding you with marshmallow turds
making it impossible not to lighten up
extricating the goo from your hair.
Give them a name
so next time you're weighed down with too serious
all you have to do is call. 6/7/22

Noticing on my June mandala several anniversaries on this day years apart, how does it not stand sterling?

A Day Inundated with Memory

Tikal,
Chartres,
Preservation Hall,
Devil's Tower—
that I experienced four revelations
on the same day years apart
marks June 8th in the swing of the year
as a day inundated with memory. 6/8/22

Here we go again.

"Change the Narrative!": 1865 and 2020

When truth is too painful,
too shameful,
change the narrative!
"Our cause was at root noble,
only incidentally about slavery!"
"They stole the election
with all those fraudulent votes!"
If repeated long enough others buy in
not inconceivably for generations.
What is truth anyway? 6/8/22

Oh for 1974 when we could at least agree on the facts.

Sure Fire Recipe

The thing about Watergate
is everyone was glued to the same tube
hearing the same facts.
The thing about Insurrectiongate
is that those with minds fortress-closed
against even innuendo against the Perpetrator
have options either for tuning facts out
or distorting them grotesquely.
Call it a sure fire recipe
for incivility to deepen, or worse. 6/9/22

Don't bow to loyal.
Ask first the bedrock question:
to whom or to what? 6/9/22

From Genesis ("Let there be light") and the Gospels of Matthew and Luke ("Be it done unto me according to thy will"), necessary partners in the only Dance there is.

Necessary Partners in the Dance

"Fiat lux!" and "Fiat mihi"—
creation and submission,
making be and letting be,
partners swaying back and forth
in the only Dance there is. 6/11/22

Anathema to True Believers.

Tao, God, Krishna, Allah—
can it all that much matter
what name we give it? 6/9/22

Sometimes a jolt is exactly what is needed.

Enough to Ignite Me into Action

After a distraught man bolted from our group
while I to whom he had bonded sat frozen,
a voice from another so jolted me
that I remember it after fifty years.
"He needs you, Charlie, and you're not giving!"
It was enough to ignite me into action then
and at frozen times since. 6/11/22

I ponder here the action in the Temple precinct, significant enough to be attested by all four evangelists.

He Had to Know Deep Down

I bet as he was overturning the tables
Jesus had to know deep down
this would have consequences,
yet he kept overturning.
Crazy man with a death wish
or man alive to a righteous fire
burn where it may? 6/12/22

The mystic's credo in a nutshell.

The Little Flower Nailed It

"Ici le bon Dieu"
drifts back seventeen years
from the basilica at Lisieux.
The Little Flower nailed it. 6/11/22

Never thought of a rounding glimpse until gazing at the Celtic cross.

Linger with What the Circle Adds

Around the familiar cross
is an encompassing circle.
Linger with what that adds,
then smile at a rounding glimpse
into Celtic spirituality. 6/13/22

I have this ready to assuage my spirit when someone gives me feedback less than glowing.

How can writers grow
if the feedback they receive
is less than candid? 6/13/22

Mary's place will always be central, even though she now for me has company.

Double Bafflement

My poems about Mary
baffle Catholics not yet released from dogma's grip
as well as those untouched by the Church
wondering what possibly is redeemable
about patriarchy's insidious creation
to keep women in their place. 6/13/22

Fond reflection on a brother just deceased, Tony Russo.

Brother Then, Now, and Forever

Back in novitiate days
we often had to speak to each other in Latin
which we gleefully murdered.
"Bonus ab" for "good-bye" was a whimsical favorite
of one who just crossed the Rainbow Bridge.
Bonus ab, dear Tony,
brother then, now, and forever. 6/22/22

For the two allusions in what follows, check out G. M. Hopkins'
"I wake and feel the fell of dark, not day" and "That Nature is a
Heraclitean Fire and of the Comfort of the Resurrection."

When Self-Laceration Holds Sway

When self-laceration holds sway
one might consult Gerard Manley Hopkins
who knew well the selfyeast of spirit
that sours a dull dough,
who could string pejoratives together—
jack, joke, poor potsherd, patch, matchwood—
but then end on a flash proclaimed twice:
immortal diamond. 6/22/22

It sounds simple, this counsel of the sages, yet it takes a lifetime.

Becoming Again Like Little Children

Listening to Thomas Moore on the subject of amulets
reminds how far we have wandered
from the magic of the first garden.
Are we really to put away childish things
or rather wake from the cultural trance
and become again like little children—
picking up special stones,
talking to living trees,
rejoining the great dance with arms
stretched wide to the sun? 6/23/22

A remarkable confession by the priest-poet Gerard Manley Hopkins: "I may as well say what I should not otherwise have said, that I always knew in my heart Walt Whitman's mind to be more like my own than any other man's living. And as he is a very great scoundrel this is not a pleasant confession. And this also makes me the more desirous to read him and the more determined that I will not."

Whitman and Hopkins: Deep Kin

Whitman's barbaric yawp over the world's rooftops
was bombastic for sure but not egotistic.
"I celebrate myself, and sing myself,
And what I assume you shall assume,
For every atom belonging to me
as good belongs to you."
Hear Hopkins chiming in with bombast of his own:
"Each mortal thing selves, goes itself,
myself it speaks and spells
crying "What I do is me, for that I came."
Not usually associated together,
are not Whitman and Hopkins deep kin? 6/22/22

Why have a conscience
if not to feel searing shame?
Why else choose to change? 6/22/22

Lamentation carries on the wind that circles Mt. Rushmore.

Mountain Sacred

Fifty years ago today
I first gazed on four pale, male faces
blasted onto a sacred mountain.
A wonder to behold
and deeply lament. 6/23/22

It turned out to be mild by comparison, still not what you want to hear.

"Guess What? I Have COVID."

Any semblance of complacence
on a Friday morning in June
was shattered by her words.
Symptoms rapidly setting in and self-test handy,
her suspicions were quickly confirmed.
But her response instead of O my God!
was simply guess what?
I'll try, still stunned, to follow her lead—
deal with it,
do what needs to be done. 6/24/22

Buddha and Jesus were onto something.

Something Deeper than Fear?

A coward lies deep
ever ready to leap
at fear's next bidding.
"Who are they kidding?" we scoff,
hearing calmness behind "Have no fear"
from the likes of Buddha and Jesus.
Wouldn't it be something
if it really were possible
to find something deeper than fear? 6/24/22

Buddha and Jesus keep haunting.

We Too Can Wake Up

Did you ever think
that behind their message "fear not"
must have been a mountain of memory
of their own prior fear?
What a comfort to know
they were where we are now
before they woke up!
At the heart of their message is hope:
we too can wake up. 6/25/22
Steady, quaking heart.
The universe has gird you
to meet the moment. 6/24/22

*Of course this will someday be reversed, that is, if democracy
prevails, but in the disheartening meantime, what unnecessary
suffering.*

Pondering Roe's Demise

The only thing originalists miss
by holding to Truth fixed forever
in documents deemed sacred—
whether Bible or Constitution—
is new truth arising
from a universe on the move.
What besides sorrow comes to mind
from this regressive Court decision?
Idolatry. 6/27/22

A half century ago but still harrowingly vivid. I smile now but didn't then.

Night of the Double Visitation

During a half century ago wild storm
somehow without breaking my neck in the dark
I made it down from Bear Butte,
soaked with wet and disappointment
having been panicked to feel something else
besides me in my sleeping bag.
When recounting my woe hours later
to one comprehending the Native way,
imagine my amazement to hear,
"You went up to pray
and the Thunderbeings literally answered!"
I think back on it now
as the night of the double visitation—
Thunderbeings answering my prayer
and something else in my sleeping bag
grateful to find shelter from the storm
but sending me frantic down the mountain. 6/25/22

The advantage of labeling a part of me Shrink is the reminder it's only a part.

Retreat is not the Only Option

"There is more to me,"
I journaled years ago in Greece,
"than that within which shrinks"—
quaint phrasing but helpful reminder
each time a new fear
triggers the part of me I call Shrink
into believing retreat's the only option. 6/27/22

My wife having recently contracted COVID, let's just say I was nervous with a new symptom.

Hmm, What's with This New Cough?

Exposed of late to several with COVID
I've been watchful for symptoms
perhaps signaling imminent invasion.
Hmm, what's this new cough this morning?
Could the little buggers have succeeded
in breaching the defenses, finding a new host?
Sometimes an active imagination
is not one's best friend—
after all a cough could just be a cough.
Then again with my history of pneumonia
it might make sense to get tested.
Stay tuned, sports fans, life's drama never ends
(until it really does). 6/27/22

Sure enough, it was my turn.

Not Enemy but Messenger

Having dodged a bullet two years plus,
I sit quietly this morning in my cathedral of trees
absorbing news received late yesterday
that COVID's bullet breached my defenses.
I choose to call it not enemy but messenger.
So what am I to learn, unwelcome intruder,
from your rude rapping on my door? 6/28/22

The poet alluded to in what follows is D. H. Lawrence.

A Torch Passed

Twenty-seven years ago this day
John Yungblut breathed his last,
readied to be, in words of a poet he loved,
"dipped again in God and new-created."
Yearning to pass a mystical torch
to those encountered on his journey,
he succeeded. 6/29/22

The context: my preparing for a big presentation. The message: be ready to stop on a dime if feedback comes in time. The reference: Harriet Tubman, intrepid guide in the night.

From Anxiety to Energy

Power Point ready—
boring if not insulting
to folks not coming not to be read to.
But blunt words from closest critic pierced the fog.
Anxiety in frying pan became energy in fire!
Harriet in the dark said "Stop,
change course now on your life!"
Thanks to closest critic (named Penny not Harriet),
I changed course in time and sing of it. 6/30/22

Recognize within you is nothing less than the momentum of close to fourteen billions years!

Your Soulforce is Needed

Whether due to troubled past,
inadequate resources,
or "I just don't have it in me,"
resist the temptation to count yourself out.
Your soulforce is needed for challenges at hand
by the very Universe! 6/30/22

My internal adversaries (until they remember they're actually dance partners) are ever at it.

Once Touched by Fire

Moose: Once touched by fire,
why in blazes do we hold back spreading heat?
Mouse: But somebody might get burned
and then what?
Moose: You've got to be kidding.
The night's dark and cold
and we have fire! 7/1/22

The context for the following was the approach of a long-prepared for (and worried about) Zoom workshop on one of my mentors, John Yungblut, that I was co-leading with a fellow visionary and friend.

Why Don't I Just Relax and Watch the Show

I'll fluctuate like crazy these coming days
before D-Day when it's all on the line,
so why don't I just relax
and watch the two of them go at it?—
Mouse conjuring up every reason to worry
and Moose exulting in a new chance to bellow! 7/1/22

There should be no doubt as to the lie in question.

Is That Really the Face You Want to Keep?

A question to those
knowing deep down it's a lie
but daring not admit it
for fear of losing face:
Is that really the face you want to keep?
Imagine showing your real one—
granted some will jeer
but wouldn't God and the universe cheer? 7/2/22

We are to follow Jesus, insisted the catechism, "like us in all but sin." A tough hill to climb were it true.

Don't Miss the Humanity of Jesus

Blessed are the remorseful.
Had the prodigal never turned back
abject with shame for his squandering,
never would he have been dumbfounded
to hear from his father on the lookout,
"All is forgiven, come let's party!"
Had Jesus never responded
to a cry in the desert to repent,
never would he have heard
words blowing him away
upon rising from baptism in the Jordan.
Don't miss his humanity—
Jesus too was a prodigal son! 7/10/22

Think journal, think memory-binder.

Spiral Notebook

Beyond a legacy to those left behind,
think of your journal as a memory-binder
calling back both awe and trepidation
on your spiraling epic journey. 7/9/22

The challenge implied
when receiving forgiveness:
"Go and sin no more." 7/10/22

I pinch myself to realize I don't have to imagine.

Imagine Entering Such a Temple

Vaulting green cathedral,
stone circle opening East,
cloud of witnesses surrounding—
imagine entering such a temple in the morning
to greet Sun's rising! 7/11/22

The following was prompted by the Thanksgiving Address, or Allegiance to Gratitude, in Robin Wall Kimmerer's Braiding Sweetgrass, a book I could not recommend more highly for a glimpse into the profundity of the Native way.

Declaration of Dependence

Make a list of a hundred things
upon which you are utterly dependent.
Call it a Declaration of Dependence,
prelude to your Thanksgiving Prayer. 7/12/22

Struggling to comprehend this will reveal how far one has wandered from the world of our ancestors.

Tangible Object to Call You Back

I wish you an amulet,
a talisman to hold in your hand,
to display in your house or on your person,
a tangible object to call you back
to an experience of power!
Indigenous peoples the world over
absolutely understand. 7/12/22

Atheists lack nil
excepting perhaps a song.
Me, I hear music! 7/12/22

Beware of Christian nationalism. This is where it can lead.

A Travesty beyond Appalling

That many actually see in a consummate mobster
the crucified Jesus
says something beyond appalling
about a current caricature of religion. 7/13/22

The following events seem unrelated, but is anything unrelated in the life of a man?

Some Days Stand Out

Fifty-three years ago today
I met with the Provincial
to declare my intention to leave the Jesuits
after ten expansive, restrictive years.
Fifty years ago today
having been putting Krishnamurti to the test
with his "nonjudgmental choiceless awareness,"
I smoked my last cigarette.
I tell you some days
stand out in the life of a man. 7/13/22

Images sometimes say what volumes can't.

No Comparing Candle with Blowtorch

The Watergate scandal
was peanuts compared to this,
candle compared to blowtorch.
Whether enough courage of conscience
remains to save the Constitution
from going up in flames
is the burning question. 7/13/22

I bet each can remember a time when the die was cast.

The Die Had Been Cast

Alea jacta est, I mused in Latin,
as I signed on this day long ago
my letter of release from the Jesuits.
I knew what was ending—
decade-long station on the journey—
but couldn't dream what was beginning.
Only this certainty—
the die had been cast. 7/14/22

Just think of it.

Bodhisattva

Imagine being so embraced by an understanding,
filled and fired by a conviction,
that you'd want to keep coming back
however many lifetimes it would take
to help everyone else get there. 7/14/22

Synchronicities—
universe not only lives
but secretly schemes. 7/15/22

Same phrase, vastly different meaning.

Choking Up

There's the deer-in-the-headlights choking up—
too frightened to think or move.
There's the heart-too-full-to-speak choking up—
holy ground here, take off your shoes.
I pray as my journey continues
to choke up less, choke up more. 7/15/22

Right up there with the timeless moments.

Face to Face with Resplendence

We headed north from Portland
to see the great mountain
fearing clouds might be enshrouding.
Around and around we climbed higher,
hoping against hope,
until suddenly we rounded a bend
and were spellbound to be face to face
with the full resplendence of Mt. Rainier!
Some moments are etched forever. 7/16/22

A final conversation with Ellen DeHaven, not to be forgotten.

In True Ellen Fashion

Wouldn't you know I forgot my earbuds
and all she could do was whisper.
Still I could make out her greeting,
"How was your summer?"
Then upon hearing of our trip to Alaska,
"What stood out most?"
Soon she had drifted to sleep
with me absorbing what conceivably could be
her final blessing.
Not a single word about dying,
rather in true Ellen fashion,
"How are you? Tell me more." 7/16/22

Imagine befriending a tree.

You Think They're Just Standing There?

You tell me trees have nothing to say,
I tell you your listening could be finer-tuned. 7/15/22

Putting myself in another's skin.

Skin Crawling

An aspiring dictator inflames millions,
armed and dangerous.
If my own skin crawls,
what if it were darker? 7/17/22

Our institutions
we blithely used to believe
will be our guard rail. 7/18/22

Tragedy breeds empathy if you let it.

Remembering a Seismic Shock

A call years ago from my mother
on a searing July day
brought the searing to my heart—
not only did my sister have cancer
but it was terminal.
A seismic shock had just shaken
ground we had assumed firm.
I pray for those around the world
this day stopped in their tracks
feeling their foundation shake. 7/18/22

Another kind of prison.

Incarceration—
by far worse than a cellblock
when locked in a lie. 7/18/22

Shape-shifting the Narrative

How pitifully artful we are
in shape-shifting the narrative
to avoid the truth of our shame
that could set the record straight
and us free. 7/19/22

What is it about this ritual, I wonder, that has for me such power?

I Have Spoken

Before passing the talking stick
to the next in the circle,
each ends calmly and strongly
with "I have spoken." 7/19/22

The fieriest of words has become tame.

Explosive Word "Conscience"

Think thunder following lightning
when hearing that explosive word "conscience."
We would be less than human
without a flashing bolt
seizing us as it were by the collar
whenever we dish out dishonor,
splitting our interior sky
with a thundering "for shame!" 7/19/22

Assorted haiku.

Whomever you meet
has come to alter your life..
Be on the lookout. 7/2022

Dog whistle sometimes,
blatant bullhorn more often —
the faithful hear both. 7/20/22

Whirlwind on the way
as two grandkids and three dogs
will keep shouting NOW. 7/21/22

Returning from trip
we find succulent buds gone—
deer have been feasting. 7/26/22

Two magical birds
hovering then swiftly gone
start the day humming. 7/26/22

Feeling my way into being 80.

Pop Pop Pondering

It likely has to do with being 80
but what if this trip to my grandkids
turns out to be my last?
Morbid you say?
How so, I say,
if it helps me to savor? 7/21/22

Lethargy too invites attention.

Paying Heed to Lethargy

With lethargy settling in
I'm wonder why.
Should I pay it no heed
content with dog in lap
and soft clatter of leaves in the rain?
Ah but as lethargy is hardly contentment
I trust if I stay with it
it'll come to me why.
Not every day feels like summer
even if it's late July. 7/27/22

Check out Yeats' On Sailing to Byzantium for the reference.

So What if My Soul Keeps Clapping

My body's in decline,
evidence is in the mirror—
chest sunken,
skin sagging where muscles had fairly rippled,
where hair had announced vigor.
A tattered coat upon a stick comes to mind—
but so what if my soul
finds reason to keep clapping? 7/29/22

Countless the ways Jung has marked me.

Winking to Jung in the Wings

Feeling cherishes past,
sensation prizes present,
intuition heralds future,
thinking weaves all three
into a tapestry stunning.
I wink to Jung in the wings
as I build my own tower. 7/29/22

July 31st is the feast day of St. Ignatius, founder of the Society of Jesus (Jesuits). The prayer at the end of his Spiritual Exercises seems an apt rehearsal for the final curtain call.

Calling Us Each to a Great Giveaway

"You've given me everything—
liberty, memory, understanding, will—
now I give it all back.
Empty of all but your love and your grace,
I am full."
So prayed the man whom we celebrate today
calling us each to a great giveaway. 7/31/22

My trip to Alaska rekindled a longtime affection.

Now There was a Natural Man

When winds pick up,
limbs start flailing,
leaves roar like waves breaking,
I think of John Muir climbing a tall tree
in order to sing with abandon
in the majesty of a mighty storm!
Now there was a natural man. 8/2/22

Never are there enough poems about Earth.

Number Three out from the Sun

Mercury and Venus, too close, too close—
fried.
Mars, Jupiter and the rest, too far, too far—
frozen.
Charmed in between is Planet Number Three,
home of our loves every one. 8/3/22

Theology put to music: Hopkins' kingfisher sonnet.

Hopkins Nailed the Incarnation

"For Christ plays in ten thousand places"—
Hopkins nailed the Incarnation!
Jesus, granted, was one of those places
but so can be the reader of these pages
crying no less than the carpenter's son,
"What I do is me, for that I came." 8/8/22

*Anyone believing Christ was the last name of Jesus will have trouble
with this one.*

The Peril of Conflation

Jesus: historical;
Christ: archetypal.
Conflate the two and open to door
to contention weaponized for war. 8/8/22

Poets were consigned
("both useless and dangerous")
to the furnace first. 8/8/22

What is it about poets and death?

Make Room on Your Left Shoulder

Death sits on your left shoulder—
cause for dread
or for mindfulness instead? 8/9/22

Can you not imagine a point of no return for democracy?

Once was Enough

Maligner in chief,
bully in chief,
inciter in chief—
a second time would break us. 8/10/22

Think not just humans
in the image and likeness
but the universe! 8/11/22

Hold onto your past journals—you never know.

Everything is Firing God

In my journal forty years ago:
"Everything is firing God!"
Not yet acquainted with George Fox,
it must have been Teilhard on my mind
or a Basque soldier centuries earlier
stopped in his tracks at Pamplona. 8/11/22

I first recognized this decades ago with John Steinbeck. Ah, but more were to come. I suspect others have their own list.

Soul Kinship

I marvel at novelists
who by taking you into their worlds
widen your understanding of your own.
Michener, Hillerman, Kidd, Kingsolver—
no other explanation than soul kinship. 8/11/22

The evidence is before our eyes.

Alas, No Longer

It used to be hard to imagine
the terror in hearts across Europe
with fascism on the rise. 8/11/22

There's a reason some rhetoric is called inflammatory.

Nobody to Blame Really

⌒

A man was shot dead yesterday
after driving to the FBI office in Cincinnati
with the intention to start killing.
Nobody to blame really—
he must have been mentally ill. 8/12/22

⌒

Ye gods that's me.

Photo just received
of my grandson hand in hand
with a stooped old man. 8/12/22

⌒

Sacred space, liminal place.

A circle of stones
in a cathedral of trees—
a pearl of great price. 8/13/22

The passage is from Vernon Ruland's Living out the Questions: A Jesuit Confession.

Courage, not Merely One Value among Many

In case you ever doubted the centrality of courage,
listen to my wise former teacher:
"Courage is not merely one among many values
but the form of every value at its moment of testing."
May whatever else we pray for each morning
we include courage. 8/14/22

In case you never considered Black Elk a mystic.

The Center of the World—Anywhere!

"Harney Peak, where you stood in your vision,
 is that the center of the world?"
"Anywhere is the center of the world."
Let this response of Black Elk
carry you through the next day
and your lifetime. 8/14/22

Here's rich ore from the mother lode.

Is not Friendship like Striking Gold?

Twenty-five years ago this evening
while staying with a friend in Colorado
he and I stood long in his yard
reminiscing about our journeys bound together
despite miles separating and years intervening.
Is not friendship like striking gold?
Wherever your journey takes you,
you carry with you gold. 8/14/22

Can we really feel loved by a deity distant?

As Close as in Your Heart

Is God looking down from a distance
wondering how you'll fare today
or as close as in your heart
figuring it out with you? 8/14/22

Navigating the sea-change not for one of us came easy.

Bewildering Adolescence

Imagine you're a teenage girl
suddenly with a knockout pair
to announce to the world.
Imagine you're a teenage boy
astounded at the force within you
rising unbidden. 8/14/22

Imagine it if you can, and I wasn't yet 18!

Cassock Day

I'll never forget cassock day
on the Feast of Mary's Assumption.
Such pride despite the discomfort
of wearing black robe in sweltering August
and white collar pinching neck.
Now I could write N. S. J. after my name
in those weekly letters back home.
No matter that said letters
following medieval custom
were read by a censor,
I now wore a cassock, bore a collar,
was a novice in the Society of Jesus! 8/15/22

One of my great joys is to have provided my father-in-law a harbor of calm after his voyage of a near century.

His Spirit Still Hovers

Eighteen years ago this morning
surrounded by a hundred roses
Penny's father breathed his last.
For nine years his kindly presence
had been sheer blessing for us all,
most especially his two grandchildren.
Fare well, gentle Milton,
your spirit still hovers. 8/15/22

Ever remember busting with a secret? Few things are sweeter.

Scheming to Spring a Question Monumental

What a rendezvous it was
in that London airport in '76—
back together after more than a month
with me scheming to spring
a question monumental
to be witnessed three days hence
by ancient standing stones.
I'd not be writing this poem
were the outcome of my scheme
not in accordance with my dream. 8/15/22

As for the aforementioned scheming...

A Belated Thank You, English Bikers

Here's a scene for you.
Tired travelers late in the day
were relieved to find lodging at the Red Lion,
English pubhouse not far from Stonehenge.
Alas bikers by the scores around midnight
converged for a raucous convocation.
Though I cursed them then
for disturbing sleep that wasn't coming anyway,
I now look back to imagine
they must have caught wind of the question
I was about to pop the next day
and the answer I'd deliriously be given.
A belated thank you, English bikers,
for anticipating forty-six years ago
a raucous convocation our own! 8/17/22

I smile to tell folks
I was stoned when I asked her—
Stonehenge our witness! 8/18/22

True Story

After the lyrical the practical—
"Yes, love, but let's move it,
the last bus is leaving!" 8/18/22

A friend who has ventured Eastward has given me something to think about.

> Why a strange notion
> if the work is unfinished?
> Reincarnation. 8/14/22

History will treat her kindly.

Refusing to Conspire in a Lie

> Thinking of a senator about to lose her job
> for daring to break ranks
> in order to shine light on a lie
> calls to mind both standing on principle
> and heeding a teacher's warning long ago
> against gaining the world at the price
> of losing one's soul. 8/16/22

Searing for a family

> Excruciating—
> a father finding his son
> dead next to a gun. 8/18/22

> Whose torment greater?
> The one pulling the trigger
> or those left behind? 8/18/22

If the name John Yungblut rings not a bell, and if you are a spirit seeker, my hope is you will inquire further.

We're Here to Imitate No One

John Yungblut loved to quote
Carl Jung's warning against imitating Christ.
We're here to imitate no one, each agreed,
in our search for the Grail of individuation.
If Jesus found the Christ by imitating no one,
by God so can we.
Good news! 8/17/22

Not seeing them doesn't mean they're not there.

Harbored in Your Heart

What if all who have loved you
having sailed out of sight
are safely harbored now in your heart
reminding you of your light? 8/20/22

How wiser than we were our ancestors.

The Power of Association

"Objective correlative" was T. S. Eliot's phrase
for the power of association.
Words of our abiding ancestors—
"amulet, talisman, charm"—
ring quaint if not superstitious to our ears,
but think of an object you treasure—
perhaps wear on your person,
display on mantel or wall,
enshrine on altar.
Strangers shrug seeing an object,
you smile from your deep heart
at an objective correlative of presence. 8/21/22

We have each a lot to ponder.

The Mystery of Things

I'll be 81 in a month,
my only sister never made it to 33—
just an old guy pondering late at night
the mystery of things. 8/21/22

Query to invite
("What's your totem animal?")
a revelation. 8/22/22

Live long enough and have like stories to tell.

A Handshake Felt Still

My brother's terse message over the phone: "Come."
I flew back to Cincy the next day
to say goodbye to my father.
Important farewells, etched forever,
are not always spoken.
A long strong last handshake
from my life's only father
my hand thirty-four years later still feels. 8/22/22

Some things you just savor.

Affirmations from a Beloved Community

One was reminded of me
while watching Leonard Cohen's "Hallelujah."
Another loves my gentleness,
seeing in me Mr. Rogers.
Yet another was unsurprised to learn
Hummingbird is my totem animal.
I'm letting these wash over me,
affirmations from a beloved community.
Mouse: But there's so much they don't know,
so carefully hidden.
Moose: They know what they see—
a poet singing, Mr. Rogers with his kind way,
Hummingbird darting from flower to flower.. 8/23/22

When you walk away
from one you have been kind to,
you've passed on the flame. 8/23/22

Just your nondescript month.

August 2022: There's No Telling

Russia's invasion of Ukraine grinds on—
no telling the outcome.
So many comeback variations—
no telling when COVID will end.
American democracy on the line in the midterms—
no telling if the perilous tilt will be halted.
Will Mar-A-Lago revelations change any minds
or even fully come to light?
Will blood soon start flowing in the streets
with so many armed and disaffected?
How will Big Oil with their DC puppets
rationalize the next climate fire?
How will those beholden to the NRA
rationalize the next mass slaughter?
There's no telling. 8/23/22

Aren't conscience and courage when it's over all that matters?

Truth's Stone in Her Sling

Liz Cheney—
David hopeless against bully Goliath?
Only if you discount the power
of truth's stone in her sling.
Guaranteed the day will come
when she will be vindicated
at no cost to her soul. 8/23/22

What beats learning that a joy deemed private is shared by a multitude?

Come Join in Joyous Cavorting

Cavorting in my solitary way for years now
with the spirit of Howard Thurman,
I thrill to learn how many others
have been no less joyously cavorting.
You who yearn for a beloved community
welcoming to every spirit-journeyer,
come join in the joyous cavorting,
come discover Howard Thurman! 8/24/22

Nothing did Howard Thurman yearn more for than the broadening of the Beloved Community.

Beloved Community

Imagine that all who have inspired you
across your ocean journey
are anchored so deeply in your soul
that they steady your bow each morning
as you steer against winds with their cheering
toward the horizon all yearn for,
then hear their salute at the end of the day
for having sailed the ship of Earth
in the homeward direction! 8/26/22

Don't be too quick to judge it anti-climatic, Black Elk's later life.

Blessed by More than One Vision

Pondering Black Elk's two great visions—
of the Hoop of all Nations when young,
in later years of Christ's Resurrection—
instead of having to choose between them
why not bow before the possibility
of a wise and holy man who was blessed
by more than one vision? 8/26/22

John Woolman was hardly a welcome guest.

When John Woolman Paid a Visit

Quaker slaveowners must have squirmed
learning that John Woolman was about to visit.
Stiffening in anticipation of reprimand,
they were relieved by his respectful manner,
plus he listened!
But when it was his turn to speak
about the burden on master as well as slave,
their squirming returned.
Could they really under a just God's scrutiny
defend it? 8/27/22

Never will I forget back in seminarian days when it was read aloud in the refectory to us, digesting between bites the thunder of it.

Required Reading for Every American

Required reading for every American—
A Letter from a Birmingham Jail.
That would be my dream
on this day 59 years after he proclaimed
to the nation his own. 8/28/22

May this from Mary Oliver's Upstream (57-8) invite you to learn which "forebears, models, spirits" she was inseparable from.

Ignore not Her Prose

You who are enamored of the poetry of Mary Oliver,
ignore not her prose. After mentioning a dozen spirit
titans in her life, listen to how she sings of their absolute
centrality:

> "Forebears, models, spirits whose influence and teaching I am now inseparable from, and forever grateful for. I go nowhere, I arrive nowhere, without them. With them I live my life, with them I enter the event, I mold the meditation, I keep if I can some essence of the hour, even as it slips away...fortifying company, bright as stars in the heaven of my mind. They were dreamers, and imaginers, and declarers; they lived looking and looking and looking, seeing the apparent and beyond the apparent, wondering, allowing for uncertainty, also grace, easygoing here, ferociously unmovable there; they were thoughtful."

Your own spirit titans traveling with you, does this not coax
you to sing of them? 8/28/22

Nature's Offer of Salvation

Mary Oliver could have written more about abuse
having known it firsthand
had she chosen to.
Clearly she decided what was needed more
was news from the natural world
offering salvation to all of us. 8/26/22

Orchestra—what great metaphor!

To Think, a Member of the Orchestra!

In the grand scheme of things
individual lives would seem but blips,
flickering fireflies in the night
on the way to oblivion.
But think if the big picture
at heart is a grand scheme,
a symphonic slow building
with each individual's contribution
adding music to the very spheres! 8/29/22

I get carried away when pondering slight tilts.

Improbable Felicities

Even with a masterful explanation
my mind has trouble grasping
the physics behind the slight tilt
in Earth's incessant eastward spin,
but my heart perfectly grasps
the result of this improbable felicity.
"If the tilt were zero
there would be no seasons."
What other felicities
in our ever-spinning personal lives
is improbably brought by each new tilt? 8/30/22

A favorite quotation: "Be kind for everyone you meet
is fighting a hard battle."

Each simple kindness
flashes a bright meteor
across a dark sky. 8/30/22

Don't the sages agree?

Finding contentment
in the plenitude of now—
happiness enough. 8/30/22

Boiling it down.

> "Can you find me here?"
> (incessant queries from God)
> "Can you love me here?" 8/30/22

∽

Paul's great metaphor: the body needs each member!

> Just think where we'd be
> without buzzards taking care
> of the carrion. 9/3/22

Is our individual essence at bottom insubstantial (as we hear from the East) or are we here precisely and substantially to bring something new to the ongoing awakening of the universe?

Bliss Doubled

∽

> "Tat tvam asi" intones a Hindu Scripture—
> thou art that,
> separation is illusion.
> I like to imagine instead
> the flute smiling to experience bliss doubled:
> both one with the august symphony
> and bringing to it a sweet note
> that no other can. 9/4/22

Best way to counteract "Woe is me"? Remember your jackpots won.

Make a List of Jackpots Won

Turn idle hour into romp
through your glittering secret stash—
make a list of jackpots won
beginning with your conception! 9/6/22

*Midterm elections coming up, normally disfavoring incumbents, this
time just might be different if Trump again throws his weight.*

Call it Dreaming

Remembering Georgia in 2020
gives me hope for 2022
even with history and pundits predicting
both House and Senate will swing Republican.
With Trump throwing his weight
behind every election-denier running,
that might just be what it takes
to confound history and the pundits
(remember Warnock!)
by swinging Senate and keeping House
in the hands of those grasping the urgency
of stemming the fascist tide.
Irony of ironies—
the wannabe king may be the very one
to save democracy! 9/5/22

The allusion is to Mary Oliver's poem, "Wild Geese."
Google it and see.

Clarion Calls

There they go, the geese,
wing to wing with Mary O's spirit,
clarion calls ever announcing
our place in the family of things. 9/7/22

To retaliate is instinctive—"we've got to stop them, there's no other
way." And yet, and yet, claim those we admire.

Wage Peace instead of War

Excruciating are the choices
when rockets split the night
and innocents are slaughtered.
How instinctive it is to retaliate in kind
to stop the brutes,
to save the innocents.
But didn't Buddha and Jesus say hold,
Fox and Gandhi and King say hold,
there's a better way
that doesn't sow seeds for further killing?
Harness imagination and heart, they say,
pray courage to wage peace instead of war. 9/7/22

A thought to start the day.

Nothing not Family

"Think of me as family."
What if this is what you heard
from everything you encountered today—
nothing from sunup to sundown,
bright day to deep night,
not family? 9/9/22

Ask about more important things.

Don't Ask an Old Guy about His Ailments

Don't ask an old guy about his ailments,
ask him about the things he most cherishes,
discoveries that have made his eyes shine,
people he holds close to his heart,
the difference he hopes he has made
in the stupendous gratuity
of the years he's been given,
the difference he hopes still to make
in whatever time remains. 9/9/22

Looking back fifty years.

Caribbean Wild Storm

It was called the flying bridge,
topmost perch on the ship
where I stood with hands gripped to the railing
bracing against the fierce wind,
exulting in the sheer force of it!
Most things fifty years ago I forget
but not that Caribbean wild storm! 9/10/22

Remembering a wild storm calls to mind Steinbeck and Hopkins.

Energies Unleashed

"There must be great violence in me,"
John Steinbeck once mused,
"to thrill so to violent storms."
Hopkins' way of catching the same:
"And glow, glory in thunder!"
What energies both unleashed
in their advancement of creation! 9/10/22

"Finding Your Roots" has moments electric.

They had *Names*

"They had *names*."
It wasn't just her voice carrying reverence,
it was her eyes and whole being
overwhelmed to have just learned the names
of those whose blood runs in her veins.
"They endured so I could thrive
and now I have names!" 9/11/22

Part of White privilege are things, some momentous,
we don't even give thought to.

Stolen

You who smile
at the feel and the sound and the sweetness
of the names on your lips of your ancestors,
imagine were your skin darker
that a mark of the system siring America
is that along with so much else stolen from you
is the feel and the sound and the sweetness
of the names on your lips of your ancestors. 9/11/22

"Bleeding heart liberals" always causes me to shake my head.

Before You Dismiss Bleeding Hearts

Before dismissing bleeding hearts,
where in the world
would we be without them? 9/12/22

Hope for hearts hardened?
Perhaps it's this simple:
let them again bleed. 9/12/22

It will be helpful to remember that as archaic as alchemy strikes the modern ear, it is all about transformation.

The Alchemist's Secret

Listening to one pour out her heart
for the world's sufferings and her own
revealed suddenly the alchemist's secret—
base metal into gold
by means of compassion! 9/12/22

I invite you to recall when the animation in another's voice re-animated something in you.

When You Hear Another Sing

I couldn't spy the sparkle
not seeing her eyes
but could hear it in her voice
when she sang of her vast admiration
first for George Washington Carver,
then for Ebenezer Scrooge!
After hearing this exclamation from her soul
I couldn't help singing of them too—
call it the alchemy that happens
when you hear another sing. 9/12/22

I can imagine Jesus shaking his head.

Noting the Challenging Message of Jesus

Do not read Bill McKibben's new book
The Flag, the Cross, and the Station Wagon
if you are resolved to hold onto privileged status.
In light of the challenging message of Jesus—
resisting rather than upholding the status quo—
would that we heard fewer boasts
about lofty Christian achievement
and more utterances that shine with humility
like this from Maya Angelou.
"It is my blessing to be a religious person.
I'm trying to be Christian." 9/16/22

Seekers, take note.

Howard Thurman's Mind, Heart and Spirit

Breadth of words wise with truth
signaling greatness of mind.
Deliberate word-cadence
grounded in the sound of the genuine
signaling greatness of heart.
Words inviting any and all
to find home in the Beloved Community
signaling greatness of spirit.
Seekers, come rejoice to discover
Howard Thurman's mind, heart and spirit. 9/16/22

Always on the lookout for metaphors.

Think of God Fishing in your Pond

Think of God as a fisher
casting each day a line in your pond
hoping to catch a whopper
of kindness or courage. 9/16/22

Nothing like taking technology to the woods.

Amplifying Forest Sounds in Early Morning

I'll admit hearing aids can be a nuisance,
but sliding a couple of bars on my cell phone
to the max degree of amplification
and suddenly I'm waiting for sunrise
in a jungle with sounds teeming! 9/17/22

Lincoln was far from an irreligious man.

Lincoln Praying

Preliminary proclamation in breast pocket,
with bated breath he awaited news from Antietam.
That he gave allegiance to no church
didn't mean he didn't pray. 9/17/22

Several making a pitch for Cloud Cuckoo Land.

Temple Library

Having just finished listening on Audible
to Anthony Doerr's *Cloud Cuckoo Land,*
I find myself beginning it again
to better appreciate the magical stitching
behind the patching together of parchment fragments into
a codex prompting you to take off your shoes
before entering the next temple library. 9/17/22

When a Book Goes out of the World

"Books like people die.
If they are not safeguarded they go out of the world.
And when a book goes out of the world,
a memory dies a second time."
You who wonder the place of books,
allow a story of an old shepherd—
turned donkey, then sea bass, then crow—
to carry you to a land in the clouds
that will sing libraries to you ever after.   9/18/22

Book Burning is Sacrilegious

Book-burning pierces the heart—
desecration of past,
theft of future. 9/19/22

Mary Oliver begins her short poem "When" with these words, anathema to True Believers: "When it's over, it's over, and we don't know, not any of us, what happens then…" Bottom line: my prognostication is as good as yours.

Anticipating the Big One

That our prior joyous reunions
might serve as dress rehearsals
in anticipation of the big one
will evoke "Poppycock!" from skeptics
who pity wishful thinkers,
but what's the harm in anticipating
something beyond the Rainbow Bridge?
Pie in the sky
beats disappearing into nothing. 9/18/22

Too few, I declare, poems celebrating crows.

Raucous Caucus

Crows are at it big time—
dozens nearby in raucous caucus
electing the sun unanimously
to be President of the morning! 9/18/22

G. K. Chesterton once suggested, whimsically but wisely,
that we ought to place a skeleton on each dinner table, which
invites this haiku.

> Let skull on table
> augment the savory taste
> of each luscious bite. 9/19/22

> There's no holding back
> the stroke of midnight coming.
> Daylight, you're still here! 9/19/22

> How do I lure you?
> Coating title with cunning—
> first words adhesive. 9/20/22

Let your spirit feel in accord with the single breathing.

> Breathing in and out
> when joined by seven billion—
> holy communion. 9/20/22

117

Ever wonder where Hitler found his inspiration?

Where Hitler Found His Inspiration

That Ken Burns is a national treasure
is confirmed yet again
in *The United States and the Holocaust.*
if we ever, as person or nation,
rise to the wisdom of humility
we will acknowledge with cringing
our complicity in the very things we condemn.
Take a close look, America,
at where Hitler found inspiration
for his fiendish vision. 9/20/22

*If there's something that comes after, wouldn't time
have to come with it?*

Trying to Imagine Time's Disappearance

Time-bound deliriously,
what in heaven's name would we do
if frozen in a celestial playground?
More like hell if you ask me. 9/20/22

Birthday musing.

Thundering Thanks

I'm inclined to trust an intimation
that time on the other side
will come to no screeching halt
(otherwise would love then not freeze?)
meaning our seeming last hurrah
may well be but a prelude.
If in this I'm seriously deluded
and poof all disappears me included,
may then my last hurrah
be thundering thanks to the world
for the grace of having sat at a feast. 9/21/22

Am I dreaming or being dreamed?

Integral to a Stupendous Dream

Not for naught
has the universe been dreaming
across billions of years.
Instead of a fluke
trust you have a reason for being,
integral to a breathtaking dream. 9/21/22

Ah, the stories we each have to tell.

A Birthday Recollection

After cooking me a birthday dinner
then offering me a pleasant smoke,
a lady long ago groped to find the words
to tell me it was over.
After she thanked me profusely
when my empathic response caught it perfectly,
I remember wryly smiling
to note the productive use I was putting
my newly-acquired counseling skills.
I smile now to look back, this time not wryly,
at my wildly felicitous fortune
that one door then sourly closing
made possible but two years later
the sweetest opening of another. 9/21/22

What I'm writing with
on the subject of my friends?
Permanent marker. 9/21/22

Ever wonder why that poem has spoken so deeply to so many?

Promises to Keep

If miles to go before we sleep,
what, my friends,
are our promises to keep? 9/21/22

Frost and Oliver carry me back.

It's Where the Confidence Comes From

Robert Frost:
"We begin in infancy
by establishing correspondence of eyes with eyes."
Mary Oliver:
"It is where the confidence comes from;
the child whose gaze is met
learns that the world is real, and desirable—
that the child himself is real, and cherished."
Is it any wonder
words such as these incline me with cherishing
to remember my mother? 9/22/22

Keenly anticipating our upcoming trip to Turkey.

Anticipating Turkey

Ephesus,
where Paul preached and Mary died—
soon I will set trembling foot.
Then, steady heart,
on to Istanbul and Hagia Sophia! 9/22/22

Carl Sagan takes flight here on "perhaps the greatest of human inventions."

What an Astonishing Thing a Book Is

I'll go out on a limb
and declare no writer on Earth—
poet, playwright, essayist, novelist, memoirist—
wouldn't cheer this by Carl Sagan.
"What an astonishing thing a book is.
It's a flat object made from a tree
with flexible parts on which are imprinted
lots of funny dark squiggles.
But one glance at it
and you're inside the mind of another person,
maybe someone dead for thousands of years.
Across the millennia, an author is speaking
clearly and silently inside your head,
directly to you.
Writing is perhaps the greatest of human inventions,
binding together people who never knew each other,
citizens of different epochs.
Books break the shackles of time.
A book is proof that humans
are capable of working magic."
Long live memory of Carl Sagan,
long live funny dark squiggles. 9/24/22

Imagining wistful thoughts at the end.

Wouldn't it be Nice to have a Few More?

Unless we're taken quickly
in blinding flash or deafening crash,
we'll likely sit on the edge
of the final sheer fall-off
in dimming light and gathering haze
wondering wouldn't it be nice to have a few more
dreaming nights and gleaming days. 9/23/22

I trust readers will close their eyes and remember such a one.

Her Presence Spreads

Where goes her spirit
now that her eyes are closed,
her mouth is shut?
Into every one she loved
now imbued with her.
Her presence spreads. 9/24/22

Every now and then I feel drawn to draw a Rune.

Could I Be Better Fortified?

On the brink of a trip to Greece and Turkey
I followed a hunch and drew a Rune.
Disruption.
"Accept what occurs as necessary,
called for in your deeps
out of a pressing need for growth…
The universe and your own soul
are demanding that you do, indeed, grow."
Gulp.
But then the reassurance.
"The inner strength
you have been funded until now in your life
is your support and your guide."
Could I be better fortified
as I prepare to sail beyond the sunset with Odysseus,
cross the lintel of a house overlooking Ephesus
where the mother of Jesus breathed her last,
then enter the hush of Hagia Sophia? 9/29/22

Upon rereading Howard Thurman's Jesus and the Disinherited.

No Sadder Irony

No sadder irony—
the disinherited Jesus
co-opted by the inherited. 10/4/22

The occasion was a hawk's cry.

O to Have Poets for Companions

Hawk's declaration from on high
calls back G. M. Hopkins
("it strikes like lightnings to hear him sing"),
E. E. Cummings
("his royal warcry is I AM"),
Mary Oliver
auctioning her life to hear redbird sing.
O to have poets for companions! 9/29/22

You never know where a conversation with a stranger may lead.

Lay Down Your Arms, Catholics and Protestants

Upon hearing scuttlebutt that Ignatius and
    Calvin—
theological arch-adversaries—
when studying in Paris would steal out together
for evening escapades just possibly grounding
their later supplications for repentance,
I smile at the conceivable kernel of truth.
Knowing themselves to be sinners
(exact circumstances inconsequential),
did they not sing to their respective disciples
of the absolute availability of forgiveness?
Lay down your arms, Catholics and Protestants.
Gather to party after repenting your sins,
have you not in common the unsurpassable joy
of being forgiven? 10/7/22

Where would we be without the myths of the world?

Radiant Realization

⌒

31, 37, 65, 81—
my ages when my eyes
have been graced to greet Greece—
where Odysseus sailed on wine dark seas
returning home to his Penelope—
aglow with a radiant realization
that my own Penelope and I have been discovering
that instead of haven at journey's end
home has been the entire journey! 10/3/22

In the spirit of Zorba.

The Journey *Itself* is Ithaca

⌒

I sing of Kazantzakis
as half century ago he sang to me
of Zorba teaching us to dance
as we journey toward Ithaca
entrusted with the great secret
that instead of haven at journey's end
the journey *itself* is Ithaca.
Splendiferous, boss,
now quit talking and let's dance! 10/5/22

A place of holiness overlooking Ephesus.

Where Mary Spent Her Final Days

Today I crossed the threshold
of a house where according to legend
the mother of Jesus spent her final days
pondering things in her heart
the rest of us can't imagine.
My own mother's heart
leapt with mine to be there. 10/7/22

*Aegean Odyssey was the name of our cruise ship. The intoxicating
wind reminded me of top deck glory fifty years ago in the Caribbean.*

Top Deck of the Aegean Odyssey

O to be back with the big wind
buffeting me blissfully
as I hold fast to the topmost ship railing
exulting with eyes closed to feel its intoxication
as I sail the wine dark seas with Odysseus. 10/8/22

Entering religious life in 1959, leaving religious life in 1969, then this amazing realization in 1979.

Unmoored

Like lightning it struck me
forty-three years ago today
that I was re-entering religious life
only this time unmoored from a sheltering harbor
to sail free on a sheltering sea. 10/12/22

According to the rubrics of courtly love, nothing was holier than the meeting of the eyes.

What's it about eyes
that without using a word
speaks to us volumes? 10/12/22

Bully's bravado—
behind deceptive display
a frightened boy hides. 10/13/22

An uncomfortable memory, but those can turn out to be the best kind.

What We All Need at Times

"He needs you, Charlie,
and you're not giving!"
Frozen like a deer in the headlights
after one I had encouraged to bare his soul
bolted suddenly from our encounter group
fifty-two years ago in La Jolla,
it took those words to shake me awake
not only then but at frozen times since.
Don't we all need at times
someone to shake us awake? 10/13/22

A favorite quote from Emerson: "Every word was once a poem."
I would simply add, but usually you have to dig for it.

The Temple of Potential

Take off your shoes
before entering the temple
of the word "potential."
Dig until you find the power,
the possibility! 10/14/22

*What do you think would be the signs were the United States to turn
sour?*

Sobering Words

Ken Burns' new documentary,
"The United States and the Holocaust,"
makes for difficult watching,
calls to mind sobering words
from the memoir of James Michener:
"It would be easy,
if the United States turned sour,
to establish Nazi-like concentration camps
in almost any part of our nation
and find eager recruits to staff them." 10/14/22

Give it a try and be surprised.

Expect the Unexpected

Keen will be your attention
should at the beginning of each day
this be your mantra:
"Expect the unexpected."
Disruptions and interruptions
will then have a chance
to be blessed instead of cursed. 10/14/22

On this morning seven years back.

No We Can't Go Back!

Heading out to see the sunrise,
our small craft's sudden lurch
was sufficient to throw me backwards
into a ribs-crushing crunch,
but how pleased I am that I pleaded,
"No we can't go back
until we've seen the sunrise."
We didn't, and we did! 10/15/22

Let dawn and dusk invite imagination.

Twilight Lovers

"But with the Dawn Rejoicing"—
the name of a book read sixty years ago
comes back as I spy through the window
the sky faintly beginning to brighten.
Think of night and day as lovers
rejoicing to melt into each other
each twilight. 10/15/22

If you ever make it to Amsterdam, you must go there.

How I Trembled

My pilgrimage a half century ago
to holy places across Europe
brought me this day to Amsterdam.
How I trembled to climb a staircase
hidden behind a bookcase
to a secret annex
and then up more stairs to an attic window
where a single tree could be loved
by a girl dreaming of becoming a writer
so that some day she might leave
her mark on the world. 10/15/22

"Here I am, send me."
Are any words more daring,
more terrifying? 10/15/22

Buddha and Jesus, can you not imagine them in jail?

Wage Peace

Next time war breaks out
look for the true warriors
likely to be jailed
as would have been Buddha and Jesus
for refusing to kill their brothers. 10/15/22

Only a few days but memories to last a life.

Turkey for Me Blossomed

Guide taking us to the land of his birth
across the wine-dark Aegean;
calls five times daily to prayer
reminding of monastic ways;
amazing Roman ruins at Ephesus
where Paul came close to being stoned;
house where the mother of Jesus
pondered immensities in her final years;
towering majesty of Hagia Sophia
with spellbinding hush within.
Turkey for me blossomed. 10/17/22

I never have liked the word favorite.

A Beauty like no Other

Rather than call dahlias my favorite,
I'll just say their splash
across the canvas of our garden
is a beauty like no other. 10/17/22

Such capacity
for evil as well as good—
the human gamble. 10/17/22

Having a stone to look down on makes a difference.

Call Me a Pilgrim Enamored

Remembering the hush in my heart
to have found on this day years ago
the grave of Hermann Hesse
causes me to reconsider
whether I want my ashes scattered.
Call me a pilgrim enamored
of the hush looking down on a stone. 10/18/22

It's called active imagination.

Bend an Ear to an Ancestor

Imagine one of your ancestors
with a particular claim on your mind
(even better on your heart)
has a timely message to give you
if only you bend ear to listen.
Trust an intimation to know who it is
who is awaiting an invitation. 10/18/22

Just imagine.

Drinking from Your Chalice

Imagine the joy of the universe
drinking from the chalice of your life—
manifest grandiosity
only if you've yet to discover
who it is who's behind and within you
which could just possibly lead
to illuminating why you're here. 10/18/22

A morning plea from Zorba.

Enough with the Wailing

Do you really think the pulsing universe
on its spiraling adventure forward
wants you to wail your unworthiness
on this splendiferous new morning? 10/18/22

Looking back on my baptism.

Baptism Revisited

I find myself wondering
on the anniversary of my baptism
how a sprinkling of water on the forehead
of an infant but 28 days old
can full-heartedly be cherished
when the original intention was to have his soul scoured
of the pollution of inherited sin.
But thinking on it deeper,
were we to deep-down believe
that each was conceived not in sin but in blessing,
how better for loved ones to celebrate the blessing
than by sprinkling living water on the forehead
of this resplendent new arrival in the family? 10/19/22

Perhaps we've been looking in the wrong place.

The Better Place to Look

Perhaps the better place to look
in our search to find the Grail
is back over our meandering lives
for clues into how the Grail
has been searching to find us each. 10/19/22

Are we not each Odysseus in his quest to return home?

Mythic Odysseus Sails Again

Mythic Odysseus within us each
faces challenge after challenge,
discovers wonder after wonder,
on the long voyage home. 10/20/22

One does not forget such manner of greeting.

Gift from a Passing Angel

Eyes closed
while sitting at a peace vigil
sixteen exact years ago
I felt on my cheek
the kiss of an angel.
I swear it. 10/21/22

Empathy comes at a price, but is it not essential?

Inviting the Courage to Imagine

Listening to those whose skin pigmentation
is red, black, brown, or yellow
telling it like it is in America
to those of European descent
prompts in the latter
either the instinct to defend and dismiss
or the courage to imagine. 10/21/22

I was mesmerized in Turkey to watch a weaver do her thing.

Stunning Tapestry

Joy and sorrow,
courage and cowardice,
dream and disillusionment—
do we not each shuttle before a loom
weaving all the loose ends
into the stunning tapestry
of our singular life?
Or is it less a matter of weaving and spinning
than realizing we're being woven and spun? 10/21/22

*Quakers have a testimony of equality. They are being challenged now
to bring it down from the clouds.*

Putting Teeth into a Testimony

Equality is easier to hide behind
than equity.
Catch the difference and begin to grasp
how the latter succeeds
in putting teeth into the testimony. 10/21/22

One of the great metaphors—lighthouse!

Hardcore Lighthouse Vision

"My hardcore lighthouse vision"—
I ponder these words written in my journal
half a lifetime ago.
It was already bedrock, this conviction,
that what light in the night means
for those sailing treacherous waters
is what we are to mean for each other.
Marvel at those who have been a light in your night,
at yourself for being such a light.
Would we have a prayer
of making it through treacherous waters
without each other's light in the night?   10/22/22

Roles change over the years, thank goodness.

Mothers Now to Their Mother

When a mother's burden after long years
is heavy with more than she can bear,
her inexpressible joy is her grown children
there now to help her bear it.
Mothered by her their entire lives,
their own inexpressible joy
is to mother now their mother. 10/22/22

Not all sufferings are created equal.

No Comparison

The more you love
the more you suffer,
that's the deal,
but it doesn't compare
with the suffering of not loving. 10/22/22

The spirit journey—
preparing to say goodbye
with bright eyes shining. 10/22/22

On my mind at the time was pondering the Native way of having more than one name.

Walks with Beauty

It came to me
a quarter century ago today
that I was Walks with Beauty.
As churches have their holy days
so does each pilgrim. 10/23/22

What blessing is Death on our left shoulder.

You've Got to be Kidding

Morbid, you say, to keep before me the day
when my eyelids will close
never again to open,
when my outgoing breath
will have no sequel,
when my heart's steady beat
will beat a final time?
You've got to be kidding.
Death sitting on my left shoulder
helps like nothing in the world
to reveal the wild gratuities—
eyes that keep opening,
breath that keeps returning,
drum that keeps beating
in time with the band. 10/24/22

Beware, Ye Torchbearers

Lucifer didn't fall
for being the bearer of flaming light,
just for forgetting who lit his torch. 10/23/22

Pondering seventeen years later.

I Sing of a Legacy

The anniversary of my nephew's attempt
to rescue a mate swept overboard
with both going under
gets me wondering in awe
at the giving of the most precious gift.
I deny not a tragedy,
I sing of a legacy. 10/24/22

A grandfather here unable not to sing.

Marking Multiple Shinings

How can I not sing
of a birthing from shining Earth
of a shining granddaughter
by way of a shining daughter?
May Mari never forget
how her coming four years past
marked multiple shinings. 10/25/22

At my sister-in-law's bedside

She Then Could Let Go

Not ever will some moments
be swallowed by oblivion.
A son holds his phone
to the ear of his mother
so that minutes before expiring
she might hear her granddaughter's voice.
She then could let go. 11/6/22

After Anne had breathed her last.

Touched by Something Deep

Noting the beauty
of each jeweled bead of the rosary
laced through her fingers now unfeeling,
I asked my niece whence it came
and was reminded her mother made it.
That touched something so deep
I began to weep. 10/31/22

Two then responded.

Sacred Moment, Sacred Tears

When weeping stole over me
one came to lean softly
joining her tears to mine,
while another held my hand
knowing the sacredness of the moment.
Not one will forget sacred tears. 11/6/22

There is wisdom to be learned from those who were here before.

Trusting Something Bright was in Store

Rainbow Bridge they call it,
those on Turtle Island for millennia.
Rainbow gives the clue
they trusted something not only hopeful
but bright was in store. 10/31/22

While every age is perfect, here's a pitch for 4.

A Whirl of a Girl

Let me tell you about a girl
with many a curl
who could stuff into your hat
a hundred things she's good at
like being a terrific little sister
to her wonderful big brother
and running like a rabbit
and blowing bubbles big as clouds
and serving afternoon tea to her friends
and drawing pictures with bright colors
and riding her bike fast as the wind
and dancing like a raindrop
and sparkling like a moonbeam
and for a thousand more things
making the eyes of her parents twinkle
and the hearts of her grandparents
thrum like a banjo,
thump thump like a drum.
O I could shout into next week
about this whirl of a girl
with many a curl,
but for now I'll just say it bold,
she's Mari Finn Holland
with a mind of her own
and a heart of pure gold
who just, if you can believe it,
turned four years old! 10/31/22

Wouldn't Great Mystery be bored knowing it all in advance?

Surprises for Us Both Today

When I wake in the morning
I like imagining God's eagerness
to see through my eyes
what's never in the history of the universe
been seen exactly as I'll see it.
Surprises for us both today! 11/1/22

If we're talking Mystery, who's to say?

Again that False Dichotomy

I am immortal
by virtue of my connection
with that which will live on
carrying every vestige of what I call me.
"So you're not worried
about disappearing into oblivion,
merging with the All?"
Ah, again that false dichotomy,
the One or the Many.
Who to say with Great Mystery
it can't be both? 11/1/22

We'll forget it years hence, but much was riding on this one.

The Midterm of Our Lifetime

Two years ago today
I deemed it the election of our lifetime.
Whatever you think of Biden,
two more years of Trump
(think only of COVID and Putin
not to mention bullying, lies,
and utter disregard of the Constitution)
would have done us in.
Ah, but his minions are alive (but hardly well)
poised in next Tuesday's midterms
to reinject life into fascism's march
by reclaiming both Houses
with the Supreme Court safely in tow.
May a week from today I smile
that my crystal ball had been too cloudy
with its ominous forebodings for democracy
in the midterm of our lifetime. 11/3/22

I think of this as his lodestar.

Window into Keats' Soul

"The holiness of the Heart's affections
and the truth of the Imagination"—
dwell on these words
to feel their immensity. 11/6/22

So many are the reasons to study the Greeks.

Two Different Kinds of Time

Chronos measures passing moments,
kairos bows before the momentous.
What kairos moments in your life
stand out momentous? 11/4/22

Can't we all look back and wince?

Ten Thousand Leagues from Empathy

Overhearing one smirk to remember
his gag gift of an ointment for acne
to a girl turning sixteen
embarrassing her to tears
makes me wince to remember
thoughtlessness of my own
ten thousand leagues from empathy.
May we all look back and wince,
how else become more empathic? 11/1/22

If ever by the grace of your circumstances you are able to make it to Florence, for your soul's sake don't miss the Uffizi.

Two Paintings Stopped Time

Aesthetic arrest not quite catching it,
spellbound and transfixed come closer.
Rapt perhaps comes closest
but then all these are just words.
Despite forty-four years intervening
I close my eyes and I'm back in the Uffizi
before two paintings by Andrea Botticelli
that stopped time. 11/4/22

No wonder Memory was the mother of the Muses.

How are Museums not Holy?

In the basement of the home
of my brother John and his wife Anne
is a museum of treasures brought back
from their travels to the ends of Earth
making spirit leap to imagine the reverence
in the hands that fashioned them.
How are museums not holy
for taking away our breath
before the wonders of the world
and the artistry of human beings determined
to fashion them for our beholding? 11/12/22

Recognizing there are painful exceptions to the rule,
the rule nonetheless holds.

Never Miss a Chance to Return Home

No matter the occasion,
never miss a chance to return home
to be reminded how interwoven
are all the strands of your life.
Each visit back
not only helps you gasp once again
before the tapestry of your life
but allows for the possibility
that old strands tangled over the years
might yet with the grace of time and forbearance
begin to come untangled. 11/12/22

Pondering the imponderable.

Names for the Within and the Beyond

Presence.
Mysterium Tremendum.
Sophia.
Ah!
You have your names
for the Within and the Beyond,
I have mine. 11/7/22

Thank you, Anne Lamont

When It Comes to the Bedrock Called Prayer

Hearing of a book about prayer
entitled *Help. Thanks. Wow,*
I could only shout YES.
Whose mind assaulted by the crush of things
has never cried for help?
Whose heart inundated with blessings
doesn't thunder thanksgiving daily?
Whose spirit before continuing revelation
doesn't on eagle wings soar?
Words of course only point,
but when it comes to the bedrock called prayer
I can't in the moment think of more apt pointers
(beyond immersion in Communion)
than help, thanks, and wow. 11/7/22

Crows have a bad press. Here's a corrective.

Raucous Announcements

Crows are congregating above—
what raucous racket
with announcements to each other
or is it to the world
about hunger, delight,
and the heralding sun! 11/7/22

Where tossing and turning sometimes takes me.

Does Revelation Ever Not Unsettle?

There's a world of difference
between what's wrong with me
for being unable to relinquish worries
that rob me of sleep
and I wonder what these mind-flashings,
heart-hauntings,
might be trying to tell me.
Does revelation ever not unsettle? 11/7/22

An eclipse is an extraordinary thing.

A Face of Light Darkened

Last night I put myself in the mind
of my ancestors across millennia
as together we gazed up
in wonderment beyond words
at the eclipse of the moon.
Is there any wonder
that a face of light darkened
transfixes? 11/8/22

Thanks to my bladder
I didn't miss it last night—
the lunar eclipse! 11/8/22

When it comes to daylight saving or not, I could go either way.

No Problem Either Way

Daylight saving on the one end
means daylight losing on the other—
no problem either way
if as much as you prize light
you prize night. 11/8/22

Doubtless I would not have written this were my faith shaken.

Would It Shake Your Faith?

Would it shake your faith
had Jesus' mother been a woman
conceiving a child like every other,
or had Jesus himself been married
as was expected of every male Jew?
Or conceivably have deepened it? 11/8/22

"God has a terrible double aspect: a sea of grace is met by a seething lake of fire...That is the eternal gospel: one can love God but must fear him." (Carl Jung, 1954)

Simultaneity of Wrath and Mercy

What amazes me was Jung's surprise
to learn others struggled with his pronouncement
about God's terrible double aspect.
His words call to mind the Second Inaugural
in which Lincoln underscored the simultaneity
of the wrath and mercy of God.
"He gives to both North and South this terrible war,
as the woe due to those by whom the offence came."
Ah, but then the pivot back
to mercy undergirding, overarching:
"With malice toward none, with charity for all,
with firmness in the right
as God gives us to understand the right..."
Are not they soberly reminding us,
Carl Jung and Abraham Lincoln,
to fear as well as love God? 11/10/22

Sevenscore and nineteen years ago...

Ideal Combination

After a speech of two hours
came an "address" of two minutes.
That we remember the latter and not the former
says something about the ideal combination
of brevity with incandescence. 11/19/22

For the spirit-jaded.

Balm for Spirits Jaded

Spirit drained, covers pulled over?
Come out, look around.
Spy moon, dream with stars,
yield to flower sweet fragrance,
soothe to rain's music,
gaze with ancestors into fire,
coax purring from cat,
stand in presence of trees,
marvel at plants' homage to light,
walk barefoot in sand,
thrill to thunder,
brace against wind,
feel sun on cheek, snowflakes tickling tongue,
listen in the dark to the rhythm
of your own or your love's breathing,
yield to a child's invitation
to come out and play.
Throw off the suffocating covers,
come out, look around!
Let Nature comfort and revive,
bring you back to your senses. 11/20/22

A friend of the heart, passing sixteen years ago, abides still.

She smiles in my mind.
In the grotto of my heart
her candle is lit. 11/24/22

These next two bear witness to a treasured friend. The young boy battling leukemia in the second one is my grandson.

How We Bear Our Suffering

Be slow to rue as cruel
a stroke bringing a man to his knees
when his manner of bearing his misfortune
with such faith, fortitude and grace
brings also to their knees
those in awe witnessing it.
How we bear our suffering
gives hope to the world. 11/25/22

No Better Measure

Here's how empathy works.
When twenty vials of blood
are painfully extracted from his arm,
his heart remembers and aches
for a young boy battling leukemia.
The extent of our empathy
is the best measure of our humanity.
Is there any question
that my friend measures up? 11/25/22

Some things don't change.

Still Magnetized

"I'm magnetized by the beauty of women,"
wrote I in my journal long ago.
Still am! 11/26/22

Funny thing, memory, especially on certain subjects.

Memory from Valencia

Sitting behind her several seats on the bus
I assumed she had no idea
that I was transfixed by her beauty,
but then upon leaving
she turned to smile and wave.
How did she know?
And why do I remember
fifty years after? 11/26/22

I call it my ace in the hole.

When Discouragement Darkens

I am a treasure in the estimation of my friends.
When discouragement darkens
and ineptitude weighs down,
just the thought of them
encourages me to keep heart. 11/27/22

Who can fathom eight billion? Easier to remember One.

Eight Billion Disguises

They've calculated one born recently
is the eight billionth alive human.
Imagine disguised billionfold
God breathing a single breathing. 11/27/22

Needing to be certain what lay ahead, would we ever set sail?

The Hallmark of Human

Fifty years ago today
from Barcelona I set sail for Genoa
where Columbus too set sail.
Neither of us certain
of what new worlds awaited,
still we set sail!
Isn't that the hallmark of human? 11/27/22

Empathy carries a cost. What had it been me?

O the Weight of That Log

My heart seized to hear of it—
girl of a mere seven
standing near her chainsawing father
killed by a log falling.
O the weight of that log
for the rest of his life
on the heart of that father. 11/28/22

Tennyson's words come back haunting.

May God and Their Friends Hold Them

"Break, break, break
On thy cold gray stones, O sea!
And I wish that my tongue could utter
the thoughts that arise in me...
But O for the touch of a vanish'd hand
And the sound of a voice that is still."
What crushing will a little girl's parents
have to live with down the years?
May God and their friends hold them. 11/28/22

Then bringing it closer.

Not Without Strength from Beyond

Remembering the vivacity of my daughter at seven,
then imagining due to my negligence
losing not only her present but her future—
how could I have borne it?
Not without strength from beyond
felt through the arms of my friends. 11/28/22

What is it about strong wind?

When Strong Winds are Forecast

I love opening the window at night
even when cold
when strong winds are forecast.
Ah, to lie warmly bundled
and listen! 11/28/22

Religion is not a distant thing.

Yours Too!

My breath,
one with the Holy Spirit.
My heartbeat,
one with the heartbeat of God.
Yours too! 11/29/22

You with a Grudge against Jews

You with a grudge against Jews
while claiming to follow Jesus
forget something fundamental—
never did he stop cherishing he *was* one. *11/29/22*

Imagine Jesus
after being gassed at Auschwitz
tossed in an oven. 11/29/22

Relationships with dogs go deep.

Long Live Earth Friendships

Buckley has the cutest way
of standing on my chest
and with his tender tongue tickling
kissing my face all over.
My fingers fluffing his chest fur
then scritching behind his ears
is me kissing tenderly back. 11/29/22

But one of a thousand what-ifs.

The Wild Improbability of Me

Had my grandmother at age 12
not come under the influence of a Jesuit
and converted to Catholicism,
she and the Irish John Finn
later never would have become an item.
Just pondering before woodstove flames
the wild improbability of me. 11/30/22

Some might call it morbid.

Gazing on Myself in a Future Casket

Gazing on myself in a future casket
(having recently gazed on my sister-in-law in hers)
wonderfully focuses my mind on the blessing
of each next breath breathed. 11/30/22

I've learned I'm not alone.

Train Whistle in the Distance

Train whistle in the distance—
I wonder why it so haunts,
so comforts. 11/30/22

Consider each dream
a friendly will o' the wisp—
catch it if you can. 11/30/22

At the vital core
of the treasure of Islam—
bejeweled submission. 11/30/22

Sometimes I have to scream.

Stop Murdering Jesus

Stop murdering Jesus
with your vicious innuendos
against Jews or Muslims or Blacks
or any other you deem beneath you.
And you call yourself Christian? 11/30/22

I'm quite good at hiding it.

Instinctively to Feel Put Upon

My instinctive response
when asked to do something
is to feel put upon.
O I cover it well
with a cultivated "sure, be glad to,"
but a deep selfish substrate
resents the intrusion.
Self-absorption, where we begin,
doesn't have to be where we end,
but it's going to take vigilance,
practice,
prayer. 12/2/22

Learning of Palmer's love of Howard Thurman, I smiled to learn
whence it came, not surprised as we travel the same circles.

Indra's Jewel-Net

Rufus Jones, Thomas Merton, and the Quakers
conspired to lift the eyes of Parker Palmer
to the height of the flight of Howard Thurman.
It gets me thinking of Indra
connecting every pilgrim
in a dazzling jewel-net. 12/2/22

What is the onrush
of living air into lungs
but God's next breathing? 12/2/22

An enigmatic gem from a Yaqui sorcerer named Don Juan.

Cubic he called it,
the centimeter of chance.
When it comes seize it. 12/3/22

The Monkeys had the lyrics—"And then I saw her face, now I'm a believer." Penny and I had the experience when we first saw a photo of our daughter.

And Then We Saw Her Face

December 3, 1984—
the day we first saw her face,
believers then and ever since. 12/3/22

My pilgrimage across Europe took me to the Eternal City.

Carried by Words of Fire

How could a day not be holy
that began with words in a homily,
"God is full of feeling,"
followed by a visit to the Keats Memorial?
"I am certain of nothing
but the holiness of the Heart's affections
and the truth of the Imagination."
Just a pilgrim looking back
fifty years to the day
on moments of revelation
carried by words of fire. 12/6/22

Surprise even God.

Just Another Ho-hum Day?

Think of God's anticipation
of experiences you'll encounter today
never before encountered
in the history of the universe!
Just another ho-hum day?
You've got to be kidding. 12/6/22

Validate someone's feelings.

Without Them We'd be Robots

A half century ago on this day
the priest in a chapel in Rome
spoke in his homily about a God full of feeling.
Afterwards he brought it down to Earth
after hearing the charge in my words.
"I like how you feel!"
Is it any wonder I remember it with glowing?
We're used to hearing that feelings are fluff,
untrustworthy because fickle,
but without them we'd be robots.
Tell another today
that through their feelings you feel their soul
and they'll remember it the next fifty years. 12/7/22

You call it nostalgia, I call it remembrance.

When Bly and Barks Held Forth

No one there that cold night in Durham
will ever forget the collective charge
when Robert Bly and Coleman Barks held forth.
Thirty-one years may have passed,
but in the minds of those privileged to be there
the charge thunders still. 12/6/22

If ever in the Black Hills and searching for holy ground,
give serious consideration to Bear Butte.

Each Night a Quest for Vision

It fits perfectly in my hand,
a rock I brought back from Bear Butte
where Crazy Horse quested vision.
It helps me remember as I slip into sleep
to be on the lookout for the cargo of revelation
in the guise of tonight's dream. 12/7/22

*May each savor, if blessed to reach it, the embarking on her or his
final season.*

Anniversary of an Embarking

⌣⟶

You who love four seasons,
may you live long enough
to savor the blessing of your winter.
Nine exact years ago today
for reasons confirmed by a strong intimation
I embarked upon my own,
hopeful of fully savoring the last in the wild drama
of four extravagant seasons. 12/7/22

"The diaphany of the divine at the heart of the universe on fire."

Gaze Long Enough into Fire

⌣⟶

Gaze long enough into fire
and be swept up with Teilhard
into the universe's diaphanous heart! 12/8/22

How are Words not Fire?

⌣⟶

How are words not fire?
Just think of the truth and the beauty
they've burned into you! 12/8/22

Rather than demythologize Mary, let's remythologize ourselves.

Reconceiving Conception

What if your own conception
and not only Mary's
was immaculate?
Literalism binds,
metaphor soars. 12/8/22

Reverence is a top candidate for the holiest word.

How Far Reaches Your Reverence?

Tell me how far reaches your reverence
and I'll tell you how holy for you
is the universe. 12/8/22

What is life if not fire?

Contemplating the Fiery Sweep

Sometimes I keep a fire small
so that from its initial flaring forth
to the ash from its dying embers
I imagine I'm contemplating
the fiery sweep of my life. 12/8/22

Watch out when a document gets enshrined.

Reflections on Our Right-Leaning Court

Literalists and originalists alike
try to freeze a universe aflame
purporting to enshrine Truth unchanging
but ignore in the process that like every living thing
frozen truth dies. 12/8/22

A cargo of revelation is what David Whyte calls a dream.

Gifts Left Unopened

How many gifts under last year's tree
did you leave unopened?
What about last night's dreams? 12/8/22

A tad grandiose, I'll admit, but if you're dreaming why settle for shabby?

Perhaps Someday an Ancestor of Spirit

I'll not deny it.
I hope by words sown on page
like seeds in wild pasture
I'll become an ancestor of spirit
for harvesters some later day. 12/8/22

Check out Neil Douglas-Klotz for rich glimpses into the Aramaic prayers of Jesus.

Alaha

Musing on the melding of awe with ah!
calls to mind Alaha,
the Aramaic word for God used by Jesus.
It makes a difference knowing the word he used,
imagining his face when it sprang from him.   12/8/22

Would that there were more sermons on empathy.

Before Casting Stones

Before casting stones
on those whose sexual preference
differs from your own,
imagine being in the minority
of a supposedly civilized (nay, Christian!) nation
and feeling repeated cruel bruisings
more even against your spirit than your flesh.
In time may empathy unblock you,
unharden your heart,
set you free to beam compassion. 12/9/22

Chesterton loved to jolt into understanding.

A Skull for a Centerpiece

Chesterton suggested that to fully savor our meals
it would be helpful to have on the table
a skull for a centerpiece.
Gross! you'll likely shout
until smiling to comprehend. 12/9/22

When it comes to God, look for metaphors instead of definitions.

Soooooooooooooo Much!

Remembering the end of our nightly ritual
when asking April as I was leaving her room
"How much does Daddy love you?"
and her responding by raising arms to the sky,
"Soooooooooooo much!"
reminds me of God. 12/9/22

No prude here, just a poet.

The Trouble with the F-word

The trouble with the f-word
is that it steers away
from the allure of the delight
of the loveplay that conceived you. 12/9/22

Too much psychology can mess with you.

Before You Knock Libido

Before you knock libido
remember its multiple disguises
all making the universe tick. 12/9/22

Don't you have to ask it?

A Question for Mr. Ex-President

Mr. ex-President hoping to be next President,
what does it mean to uphold
the bulwark against tyranny
called the Constitution?
Just wondering. 12/9/22

Trying to bring a word down from the clouds.

See Yourself a Mystic

Don't look down on "mystic"
or flee from it either.
Rather consider that you're one yourself
whenever awe invades
vying with the vastness
of your thanksgiving and kindness. 12/10/22

Stepping back for the big picture.

Hardly Wandering Willy-nilly

By definition all of a piece,
the universe across billions of years
has hardly been wandering willy-nilly.
As for where exactly it's heading
beyond an inclination in the direction of love,
perhaps not even God knows.
As for the fate of the Earth,
that's where humans come in. 12/10/22

*I remember being strangely relieved long ago to hear an unofficial
diagnosis from my primary care doctor.*

Being a Worrier has Helped with Empathy

My doctor might have fetched something weighty
out of a bottomless DSM-III bag
but I'm grateful he didn't.
All things considered,
"worrier" has been easy to live with
across the forty-eight subsequent years—
besides he hit the nail on the head.
It has also helped considerably with empathy
given most of the folks I've run across
are not unacquainted with worry. 12/10/22

Amazing the different takes on Jesus upon whom can be projected just about anything.

Megalomaniac or Wise Elder?

Was Jesus a megalomaniac
with all those I AMs
or simply a wise elder
issuing an invitation to the rest of us
by holding up a mirror,
a mystic who had discovered the secret
why lilies neither toil nor spin
hoping to draw us in. 12/10/22

Superficial comparisons notwithstanding.

When it Comes to Democracy

Walt Whitman and Donald Trump—
when it comes to democracy
could two names be representative
of further extremes? 12/10/22

How hard to be truly open, particularly if you're looking to critique.

Insipid at Best

⌒

If looking to criticize
you'll absolutely find something.
I've been thinking of the Democrats of the day
judging Lincoln's brief words at Gettysburg
insipid at best. 12/11/22

Some efforts give particular pleasure.

Rebels Mother and Son

⌒

In her final days
before fog rolled in to blur the edges,
Mom smiled to remember how back in college days
she of all in her class had been "the romantic rebel."
At her bedside near the end
the heart of her own rebellious son
leapt to listen to the lilt in her voice
as she quoted her beloved Keats:
"A thing of beauty is a joy forever."
You'd have to know my mother's love of beauty
to begin to comprehend.
United where it most counted
were rebels mother and son. 12/11/22

A flash of insight into what my mother passed to me.

What an Amalgam was My Mother

What an amalgam was my mother—
simultaneously called when a young girl
by her frightened mother in a storm
to light candles before a statue of Mary
and by an exultant father to join him on the porch
to listen to the glorious thunder! 12/11/22

If only we grasped it.

Each a Unique Facet

What dazzling—
to be a unique facet
of an immortal diamond! 12/11/22

What's the object of a spirit journey if not this?

Fruit of the Spirit Journey

Trust it will come,
the courage you will need
to meet the next challenge. 12/11/22

Pondering eyes on the screen.

Zoom Reflections

Eyes of each face on the screen
one day will close—
what joy they're still open
to beam out a presence
unique in all the world! 12/11/22

Looking back fifty years.

Pilgrimage Including Crete

Gazing on the very desk where Nikos Kazantzakis
wrote Report to Greco and Zorba the Greek,
books electrifying my spirit,
then on to the holiness of his nearby grave—
my reason for including Iraklion on Crete
in my pilgrimage across Europe.
Don't spirit seekers everywhere
have pilgrimages they'd love to make? 12/11/22

What endowment a conscience!

If Ever Reason to Bow and Tremble

Bring down from ethereal heights
the scrutiny of God.
Bow and tremble
before your inscrutable conscience. 12/11/22

It should not be hard to feel empathy for Mary Todd Lincoln.

Too Deep a Dive into Darkness

Mary took too deep a dive into darkness
to ever come back
but at least she had in the quiet of her memory
that last carriage ride with Abe
and, o, her sweet Willie. 12/12/22

Come meet the newest member of our family.

He'd Steal Your Heart Too

With the tawny coloring of a lion
and the face of a little fox,
our Pomeranian Buckley if you knew him
would steal your heart too. 12/12/22

You can guess the story behind this one.

Finally Getting the Point

Sometimes it takes a shout
to make the point clear,
"Paring knives are for food only!" 12/12/22

Intolerance comes in many guises.

"I'm Trying to be a Christian"

Those tempted to jettison "Christian"
for the grotesque perversions accruing to it
manifestly incongruous with the spirit of Jesus
might remember Maya Angelou
for whom the word sang.
"It is my blessing to be a religious person.
I'm trying to be a Christian." 12/13/22

Civil Rights Movement—
it proved Christianity
could be relevant. 12/15/22

It's really not complicated.

Why I Write

Words I write now
years down the road
might comfort a heart,
might light a fire.
In case you wondered why I write. 12/14/22

I still glow from our recent trip to Turkey, which included awed hush in Hagia Sophia!

Islam's Treasure

At the ruby heart and sapphire soul
of Islam's diamond treasure:
submission. 12/15/22

So many are a dog's blessings.

Soft Reverie before Fire

Soft reverie before fire—
Buckley in my lap,
all of us in God's. 12/15/22

We can't be the only ones who love to be called by name.

Call Her by Name

Sophia,
Isis,
Kwan Yin,
Earth Mother,
Mary—
the divine feminine too
loves to be called by name. 12/15/22

It wasn't so easy to be philosophic back then.

Conned by a Pro

My arrival in Israel began on a sour note.
It was fifty years ago today
when I waited in vain in a Haifa station
for a young Israeli named David,
most friendly on the ship from Greece,
to return with the repayment of my loan
that enabled him to come home.
Ah, these innocents abroad.
My gullibility slowly settled in —
I had been conned by a pro.
In the short run I clearly was the sucker,
in the long run I wonder. 12/16/22

Fire was the subject of these next three.

Fire guttering low
after earlier blazing—
I muse on my life. 12/15/22

As Any Fire-builder Knows

Too much too fast
snuffs out tiny flame.
If you aspire to spread fire,
build slowly. 12/16/22

I have to believe
along with revering trees
Druids revered fire! 12/19/22

An inkling into what's coming, for many already here.

Dread Bordering on Panic

In a pique at recent cluelessness on my part
she put it starkly,
"What are you going to do if I die?"
What it gives me is a glimpse
into dread bordering on panic
within hearts of the aging
at the prospect of one relied on
going first. 12/17/22

Context is everything.

Naked until Clothed in Context

Stroke calls to mind things divergent—
cat purring under fingers caressing,
a brain altered in a flash.
Words stand naked until clothed in context.
Upon learning about my friend,
what leapt to mind upon hearing stroke
was the opposite of purring. 12/17/22

The occasion was learning a friend had just been immobilized by a stroke.

Batter Up!

Little thought we give
to the intricate architecture of the brain
until lightning strikes to alter the wiring.
So much we take for granted
until suddenly with the next pitch
it's a whole new ball game.
Batter up! cries the umpire we call life. 12/18/22

Mindful of the sun far more than we, how transfixed they must have been, our ancestors, to anticipate then behold the solstice! Their prayer is we join them.

Transfixed before the Solstice

Never does the sun more astound
than when it stops in its tracks.
No wonder our ancestors were agog
when twice in the swing of the year
the ever-mobile source of their life
first stopped moving,
then reversed course!
Our spirits sleep if they don't leap
with our ancestors at the solstice. 12/18/22

Find deep in yourself
(Howard Thurman's wish for you)
a cascade eagle. 12/17/22

Take some time with this one—it gets to the core. What belongs on your highest altar?

The Nerve Center of Your Consent

To what do you affix the seal
of the fullest measure of your authority,
the nerve center of your consent?
Only this according to Howard Thurman
gets past the angel's Flaming Sword
on the altar in the center of the island
in the middle of your inward sea. 12/19/22

Haiku don't usually have a title, but perhaps this one will be helpful.

Imagination

Ponder it for years
and have only just begun
mining its treasure. 12/19/22

The next two were written decades apart but some things don't change. Both get to the core.

Likely No More Important Question

Whatever grace means to you,
is there room for it in your universe?
Likely no more important question. 12/19/22

Cramped or Spacious?

If you want but a single question
the answer to which more than anything else
will reveal the kind of universe—
cramped or spacious,
menacing or indifferent or friendly—
in which you live and move and have your being,
ask yourself if you believe
in any kind of gracing. April 1987

Reminding folks of an option.

Lineage

For bloodline,
check out ancestry.com.
For spiritline,
check out who has called you alive,
struck in you fire. 12/19/22

Some wisdom haiku.

> Wise ones always are
> what we're told to grow out of—
> impressionable. 12/19/22

> We'll have become wise
> when we're no longer afraid
> of being called foolish. 12/19/22

> The Magi were wise
> to decide which gift to bring,
> to trust then their star. 12/19/22

Perhaps the guard rails will hold after all.

Inching Closer to Existing

> "America is the best idea the world has ever had
> but it doesn't exist yet—
> it's a song yet to be written."
> Hearing these words from Bono
> in a recent conversation in a cathedral
> on the very day an ex-President
> was referred to the Department of Justice
> for conspiring to defraud democracy
> gives hope that the idea of America
> just inched closer to existing. 12/20/22

Parenthood never ends when comfort is needed in a storm.

May She Feel again Rocked

Overhearing my daughter's sobbing last night
having just received deflating news
that Brewster's levels were still down
perhaps calling for yet another biopsy
in his grueling battle with leukemia
was wrenching.
Tomorrow being the solstice,
I pray we'll soon experience
a swing back to the light.
In the meantime may April feel
as she did long ago when it stormed
her mother hovering close
while rocked in her daddy's arms. 12/20/22

Keeping White kids dumb
so their feelings won't be hurt—
you call this history? 12/24/22

Imagine does not mean to dwell.

Precious is Each Day

It's agonizing to imagine
those stuck in their cars freezing to death,
so why do I?
Maybe because it could have been me
suddenly on the desperate brink,
sinking into silent shriek and final prayer.
Precious is each day
that could, poof, be our last. 12/27/22

Anniversaries help us remember.

This I Absolutely Know

Twenty-seven years ago this morning
Mama's spirit took flight
to the far reaches of the universe
(who knows where?)
and the near reaches of my heart
where (this I absolutely know)
she has resided since
and forever will. 12/28/22

A moment out of time.

Half Century Ago Ecstasy

Imagine climbing a hill in the morning,
New Testament in back pocket,
unsure what you'll see from the top
when, crest reached, you look down
not only on sprawling Tiberias
but the vast sweep of glistening water!
Having read from my youth of it,
now spread out as far as eye could see—
the Sea of Galilee!
"Come, I will make you a fisher of men." 12/28/22

The next two touch on the bane of exclusivity

Capitalization Bias

Polytheism, many gods,
monotheism, one God—
note the capitalization bias.
Honor plurality no less than singularity
and what awesome array
of holy names then! 12/28/22

False dichotomies plague us.

Why not Both-And?

Instead of either-or
inviting war,
why not both-and
where each can stand? 12/28/22

On the very hillside.

A Sermon for the Ages

Marinated in Jesus juices all my life
I glow to remember back fifty years
when I stood on the very hillside
where he preached a sermon for the ages. 12/29/22

It's a holy undertaking to sum up another's legacy, particularly if the other is your mother.

She Left Me Rich

Title of my eulogy for my mother:
Legacy of Beauty.
I am the richest of men. 12/30/22

Ruminations can be triggered by the smallest thing.

Like a Trusty Pen

I never knew I had such affection for a pen—
its feel in my hand,
the ease of its flow—
until it ran out of ink.
Of course I'll find another
(I just did)
but not with that same exact feel,
with that same easeful flow.
This gives me a hint
of what lies ahead for my heart
with its affections in the tens of thousands
when it's time to let go
of far more than a trusty pen.
Hmm, it's not the same
but this new pen too
fitting not uncomfortably in my hand
has a flow of its own.
Maybe it will be sort of like that
when my body runs out.
You never know.
All I can do in the meantime
like a trusty pen
is to try as long as I can
to stay in the flow. 12/30/22

You have to admit we came close.

Two Towering Events of 2022

Two events in 2022 tower above all others
for citizens of America.
First the January 6 commission
highlighting in nine riveting sessions
the plot coming appallingly close
to dismantling our democracy.
Second, the mid-term elections
demonstrating enough were paying attention
to bring us at least temporarily
back from the no-longer-unimaginable brink. 12/31/22

Beginning this practice in 1981, I here invite others to consider the potential merits.

Yearly Mandala Serving Remembrance

Think at the end of a year
of filling a large circle
with revelations from each month
and the year's theme in the center.
Not easy remembering
without help from calendar or journal,
but imagine, were you to give it a try,
the joy of gazing upon a mandala
highlighting a year like no one else's! 12/31/22

CHARLES C. FINN

I wonder what strife
will come this year in disguise
to call forth new life? 1/1/23

*The next couple relate to a memorable game between the Buffalo
Bills and the Cincinnati Bengals, suddenly forcing perspective.*

Poem Running Down Cheeks

If poetry has something to do
with struggling to find words
to attach to profound experiences,
then in Cincinnati last evening
tens of thousands in person
and millions watching on TV
suddenly in their silence became poets
unable to find words.
Likely the most poignant poem
was running down the cheeks
of a young man's teammates
shocked by his cardiac arrest
into remembering there are things
more important than a game. 1/3/23

Reverence for life
in the unlikeliest place—
stadium turned church. 1/4/23

May bitterness in another call from you compassion.

> Bitterness signals
> rage seething unabated
> under the surface. 1/2/23

Dress rehearsal?

I Have Spoken

> Hearing from a friend
> of his twenty-six year participation
> in a talking-staff council
> stirs my imagination.
> To think of sitting with trusted friends
> while each speaks from deep soul
> then ends with "I have spoken"
> before passing the staff to another.
> Perhaps that's what we say
> before crossing the last bridge.   1/5/23

Peter nailed it.

True Now as Then

> The closest I got to Mt. Tabor
> was to see it in the distance at sunset
> fifty years ago today.
> True now as then its transfiguring message:
> "It is good that we are here." 1/5/23

Several relating to epiphany.

Epiphany

Some speak of the Epiphany,
others of having an epiphany.
Contend not over distinctions,
rather go to your quiet place, sacred space
and savor the sound and the feel of the word
as you invite to leap from you light. 1/6/23

On the Epiphany of all days.

Two years to the day
the nation's experiment
came close to ending. 1/6/23

Speaking of epiphanies...

Tourist Struck Dumb

There I was
tourist struck dumb
to be in Hagia Sophia
at time of evening prayer.
Such blessing to be struck dumb. 1/6/23

A whimsical thought that maybe birds each morning are gob-smacked with wonder to see the dramatic sky-change.

> The sky is bluing,
> no wonder birds are singing—
> black is birthing blue! 1/5/23

I can't resist a new book on Lincoln.

Book for Your Cascade Eagle

Jon Meachum's And There Was Light
will make the cascade eagle
in democracy-loving hearts soar! 1/8/23

Would you rather be loved or beloved? Here I tease out a difference.

Beloved

I'm struck by the difference
between "loved by God"
and "beloved of God."
What is it about "beloved"
that both softens and seizes? 1/9/23

Putting aside your possible quibble about the word "God," how would you answer?

Making God's Heart Leap

What action of yours
would make God's heart leap?
Wouldn't it have to have something
to do with kindness or courage? 1/9/23

You remember the exact place, even small details, when lightning strikes.

No Telling where Revelation might Strike

I received a revelation
eleven years ago this day
in of all places McDonald's
while reading about Thomas Merton
between bites of a fish sandwich
and slurps of a McFlurry.
In a flash I recognized what I knew
to be the great heart theme of my life.
Never underestimate where revelation
like lightning might strike. 1/9/23

Thinking about the prayer of St. Francis.

Did Francis not Nail It?

Generosity's endless outpouring,
not only personal but kindred—
Brother Sun! 1/9/23

When it comes to spirit, it's been downhill since Descartes.

Hubris in a Nutshell

Isn't it curious
that "animated" is valued
for connoting spiritedness
while "animism" is scoffed at
for spying spiritedness everywhere?
Could eons of ancestors
just possibly be wiser than we?
Hubris in a nutshell:
only humans have spirit! 1/10/23

Sadly even when spelled out, the words barely hint of fire.

OMG—No Hint of the Power

OMG.
Abbreviations are handy but impatient—
a quick nod so folks catch the drift
(do they even catch that?)
before rushing on.
But what of the power inherent in the words
abbreviated in the rush past the meaning?
O MY GOD.
Granted spelling out slows down,
ah, but then just maybe
a hint of the power! 1/10/23

Do something to make a small difference—has it ever failed?

Inroad into Futility

Next time you're crushed under a load—
feeling it's all futile—
do something to make a small difference.
Suddenly the load is incrementally lightened,
the whole enterprise a feather less futile. 1/10/23

"Taking for granted" always calls G. K. Chesterton to my mind, ever exhorting to take with gratitude instead.

What's on the Table is the Feast

To take for granted
is to rush past what's on the table,
hungry for distant delectables.
To take with gratitude
is to slow down and savor.
What's on the table is the feast! 1/10/23

Years from now we'll forget the meaning, but for now it's transparent. Dictators hang with dictators.

Comfort for Bolsonaro

Bolsonaro is hanging out in Florida
while fellow insurrectionists
are being rounded up back home.
Doubtless he feels comforted
to be close to Mar-a-Lago. 1/10/23

The comparisons will be offensive to some, but are the signs not painfully apparent?

On Grand Display

On grand display in the Grand Old Party
is what happens when backbone bends,
bowing before a bully.
We need no longer question
how Hitler, Mussolini or Mao
managed to do it. 1/10/23

You blessed to have an anam cara, John O'Donohue's phrase for a soul friend, will understand this one.

Carried on High Thermals

Talisman,
amulet,
sacred object—
flashing power to those who can see,
singing mystery to those who can fathom.
Gathered across a pilgrim's lifetime,
each calls forth reverence.
Imagine the joy of spirit brothers
gathering to share with each other
meanings behind each sacred object.
Carried on high thermals eagles soar! 1/11/23

Right before our eyes, is it not happening?

They Call Themselves Patriots

Obstructionists,
iconoclasts,
nihilists—
they say they're tearing down
in order to build up—
so what if the collateral damage
is democracy. 1/11/23

"What is essential is invisible to the eye."

Inscription on Her Arm

I know a woman
not the tattoo type
who nonetheless was so enamored of words
from a wise fox to a little prince
about how to tame his shy rose
she had them inscribed on her arm.
Fellow shamans understand
as does every wise fox,
little prince,
and shy rose. 1/11/23

Climbing a ladder
means wrestling with an angel,
wounding guaranteed. 1/10/23

It doesn't take much to call to mind exemplars of spirit.

My Dog Evokes Keats and Thoreau

Buckley licking my hand
then chewing his bone
calls to mind Keats and Thoreau.
Bow to the holiness of your heart's affections,
said the one.
Said the other, Find your bone. 1/13/23

Try to get your head around this one from Teilhard.

Intense and Incommunicable

"Each is our own little microcosm
in which the Incarnation is wrought independently
with degrees of intensity
and shades that are incommunicable."
Recall but a single deep relationship
layered with the nuances
of your mutual affection over multiple years
to receive a glimpse into Teilhard's understanding
of the intensity and the incommunicability
of your own distinct in all the universe
enhancement of Incarnation! 1/13/23

Likely we never stop wondering.

Old Guy Looking Behind and Ahead

I saw a double rainbow over Jerusalem one day
a half century ago when wondering
what in the world will become of me—
would I ever find a path to follow,
the right woman to walk it with?
I smile to look back on both path and woman found
but still on the lookout for double rainbows
I continue to find myself wondering
what in the world will become of me? 1/13/23

It doesn't take a Sherlock to read the tea leaves.

Upheaval Up Ahead

How can there not be upheaval up ahead
when those locked in a lie are armed to the teeth?
It reminds me of Jefferson's warning
of a coming firebell in the night
given the embeddedness of human chattel
in a republic founded on the proposition
that all men are created equal. 1/13/23

Such sounds when you listen.

Soft Symphony

Chimes ringing,
logs crackling,
humidifier humming,
air entering then exiting lungs—
soft symphony on a kind morning. 1/13/23

If you only arrive in time to see the sunrise, you've missed half the show.

Dawn's Coat of Many Colors

Array of raiments
in dawn's opulent wardrobe
to welcome king sun. 1/13/23

Years ago it was my cat Smokey, now my dog Buckley has taken his place.

Cozy Undulation

With sleeping dog under writing pad,
scribbling before woodstove fire
glides softly if not even. 1/15/23

See what you started, Rilke?

Riffing off Rilke

"In the hearts of human beings
is where God learns."
What could Rilke have been thinking
to imply God can learn?
But then this from St. Paul:
"I live now, not I, but Christ lives in me."
How then a separate me?
Hopkins jumps in: "The just man...
acts in God's eye what in God's eye he is—
Christ—for Christ plays in ten thousand faces..."
Rilke, Paul, Hopkins—are these crazy fools
or onto something incandescent?
Add Joseph's response to the question,
"Mr. Campbell, do you believe Jesus was God's Son?"
"Not unless we all are."
The riff trails into silence
after a finale from the Upanishads,
"Thou art that."
No wonder jazz is so enamored of riffing,
and Hummingbird mind so enamored of jazz. 1/14/23

Perhaps we're here to bring angels down from heaven.

Like Gabriel Carry Your Message

Everything you imagine an angel to be
is in fact (not fancy!) what you can be
when you take another under your wing.
Think who it might be,
then like Gabriel carry your message. 1/16/23

Assorted haiku.

"Racism" at core
was to justify slavery—
as ugly as that. 1/15/23

Improvisation—
after jazz think universe
and what you might add. 1/15/23

Imagine the pain
in the heart of nihilists,
the hope now extinct. 1/17/23

The quote is from Joseph Campbell.

"Beware the Error of the Found Truth"

Pray for discernment—
acknowledge that what you lack
are all the answers. 1/15/23

Never will I forget where lightning illuminated the landscape,
and a novel that paved the way.

I Just Possibly Might Have Found One

I will never forget
words rising from the silence that morning:
"Way will open."
Electrified I returned home
from my first Quaker Meeting for Worship
to write in my journal, "That's Taoism!"
God and Tao had seemed for years
contending like lion and lamb,
but on that long ago Sunday morning
in a side chapel at Hollins College
both felt at home.
Speaking of home
I sensed in my search for a faith community
I just possibly might have found one. 1/16/23

Wealth Found in a Novel

Novels can be life-changing.
What got me to my first Meeting for Worship
was reading in The Peaceable Kingdom
about the elemental convergence of the spiritualities
of Quakers and Native Americans.
What I heard rise from the silence that morning
confirmed that it pays to pay attention
to a novel striking the right chords. 1/16/23

First of all, can we agree "global warming" is not a sufficient shake?

Whether We Become Blight or Blessing

While I can't imagine a mother
ruing enough the behavior of her children
to wish them extinct,
I can imagine her shaking them with firmness
for playing with matches near a gas tank.
Whether we become blight or blessing
to the Mother we call Earth
is entirely up to us,
but some shaking with firmness would help. 1/17/23

"Child of God" is pretty radical when you come down to it.

I Am Who I Am

Just imagine hearing
from everyone you encounter today,
everything your eyes light upon today,
"I am who I am."
But only God says that, you protest.
Precisely. 1/19/23

I love imagining Rumi dancing with trees and Mary on his mind.

Rumi in a Trance

Looking out on trees swaying
calls Rumi to mind.
"The wind is the Holy Spirit,
the trees are Mary."
Be it done unto me
according to thy will. 1/20/23

One would have to be of a certain age to remember Alfie's plaintive query.

Answer to Alfie

Thinking of the word diehard
(football fandom on my mind)
gets me wondering what would it mean
to die easy.
Perhaps, old friend Alfie,
that's what it's all about. 1/22/23

Gnarled hands are a poem.

Remembering Their Colossal Service

If you're getting to be of a certain age
and look down at your hands,
you'll be forgiven an involuntary shudder
remembering their prior shape—
fingers uncrooked and unaching,
skin smooth and spotless—
hitherto taken for granted.
What a chance now to study them closely
remembering their colossal service. 1/23/23

Further musing on the Bills-Bengals game abruptly stopped in its tracks.

Suddenly Gaining Perspective

In no way to detract
from the role prayers may have played
in Damar Hamlin's recovery,
but let's not ignore the part played
by medical science and first responders.
While on the subject of miracles,
perhaps the greatest that evening in Cincinnati
was when millions across the land forgot football
suddenly gaining perspective. 1/24/23

Mari likely will not remember it, but I always will.

Butterfly Lullaby

My granddaughter of four
sang to me last evening
a butterfly lullaby
so spontaneous and tender
that my heart holds it close
like a cocoon with a secret. 1/29/23

Marveling at a force of nature.

Tsunami of Love

How could Jesus
not have been a force of nature,
a tsunami of love across millennia still spreading.
Has the living water reached your shore?
You'll know by your response
to the least of these. 2/1/23

Too few are there poems about friendship.

Friends are like Flint

Friends are like flint
guaranteed when reunited
to spark not only into warmth
but fire! 2/1/23

A query to consider as each month begins.

Before the Clean Canvas

A new month begins.
What will it take by month's end
to look back in keen satisfaction
at something to show for it?
Before the clean canvas
become Vincent dreaming. 2/1/23

Call it a journalist unabashed about his bias.

Had They Only Been Recorded

Think of the ecstasies forgotten—
illuminations, piercings, wild vistas forgotten—
that could have been put in the service
of the Mother of the Muses
had only they been recorded. 2/2/23

Smile to imagine
Memory never being caught
without a journal. 2/2/23

The vast human heart
granted is made for sweetness
but don't forget fire. 2/4/23

Would you be here if you were unworthy?

God Interrupting

"Shut up and let me love you,"
says God to interrupt
all who can't stop mouthing,
"How unworthy I am." 2/4/23

God and my dog sometimes make it clear.

Time to Stop this Navel Contemplation

When my dog rises from my lap
to stand on my chest
and look me straight in the eye,
I get the distinct impression
it's time we put an end
to this navel-contemplation.
A slight shake of my head
sometimes buys me a minute more,
but a paw in my face this morning
allowed no more procrastination.
Sometimes God makes clear
it's time to shake a leg! 2/4/23

A revelatory juxtaposition.

Alas Joined at the Hip with Alleluia

When I look back fifty years
on an exclamation in my journal
summing up the seeming incongruity
of feelings within me at the time—
"alas and alleluia!"—
I'm struck with realization bordering on epiphany
that these will ever be partners
in the only dance there is. 2/4/23

Don't wait till it's too late to tell them.

Core Shining Gifts

Three years ago today
I gave a eulogy for my brother
fastening on steadfast and playful
as his core shining gifts.
It gets me thinking
that important ones in my life
might like to hear while they're still able
what one connected at the heart
considers their core shining gifts. 2/5/23

Never had I heard of her, but does she not speak truth?

Best Armament against Propaganda

Humility, according to Evita Ochel,
is the best armament against propaganda.
"Until you realize how easy it is
for your mind to be manipulated,
you remain the puppet of someone else's game."
Truth coming at a cost to self-delusion
breeds liberation. 2/5/23

How tempting to turn the TV off.

Keeping up with the News

It exacts a price from the heart
this keeping up with the news—
presently it's earthquake devastation
in Turkey and Syria,
then there's Ukraine's daily crushing.
How can a heart not be pierced
to think of the children? 2/7/23

A fiery memory from LA's Huntington Library.

Script Forged by Fire

In the shrine-darkened library
trembling before script forged by fire
I looked down on resolute words
penned by Frederick Douglass:
"Unchain that Black hand!" 2/7/23

Do we ever stop and think about the displaced?

Terrifying Words

Could there be words more terrifying
for those dwelling for generations
on their ancestral sacred land
than those on the banner of the newly arriving—
such as MANIFEST DESTINY
or OUR PROMISED LAND? 2/8/23

Never a silence more intent.

Earthquake Aftermath

Frantic workers in the rubble
at intervals all stop
to listen. 2/9/23

Easier said than done, but it helps to be ready.

When Next Encountering Belittlement

Escape if you can
the toxic touch of those
whose default position is belittlement.
Short of escape find your voice
next time you feel the toxicity,
Stop, I find it offensive! 2/8/23

From library shelves
lest he trouble our children
remove the Baptist! 2/9/23

Things springing to our lips speak volumes.

O My God

While I cringe when OMG
is bandied about as mindlessly as Holy Cow,
I'm heartened to see
how spontaneously it springs
in circumstances both breathtaking and devastating
to the lips of so many.
Vincent's old man comes to mind
with his head lost in his hands
as he cries, I imagine, "O my God." 2/10/23

*To paraphrase Howard Thurman: "What is at the nerve center of
your consent, the core of your will, behind which you stand with the
full weight of your authority?"*

Find out what for you
burns white-hot incandescent—
why else are you here? 2/11/23

Take a year or two with this one.

Striking Declaration

"We are in the deepest sense
the victims and the instruments
of cosmogonic 'love.'"
Carl Jung's striking declaration
near the end of his autobiography
invites long pondering on the latent power
in both "victim" ("one that is acted upon")
and "instrument" calling to mind Loyola's phrase,
"instrumentum conjunctum cum Deo."
Save your deepest pondering
for what Jung means by "cosmogonic love." 2/10/23

*It seems to me you have to have become jaded not to recognize the
sterling life of Jimmy Carter.*

With His Life Jimmy Answered

Entering hospice care
he is ready to lay it down.
One embarking on a Vision Quest
asks "How am I to serve the Earth?"
I can imagine Jimmy Carter
once upon a time deciding
to let his life be his answer. 2/18/23

I wonder if this crossed Frost's mind too.

Without Promises to Keep

I wonder if the snowy woods
would be quite as lovely, dark and deep
were there no promises to keep. 2/20/23

Let's bring "mystic" down from the clouds.

Could it be that Simple?

If "mystic" feels too murky,
too presumptuous,
how about "mystically inclined" instead—
open to awe,
grounded in gratitude,
leaning into kindness.
Could it be that simple? 2/20/23

The Name of this Religion is Democracy

All humans are created equal.
E pluribus unum.
With liberty and justice for all.
The name of this religion is Democracy
with sextons Whitman and Lincoln
ringing bells in the steeple. 2/22/23

Musing on the bad press crows usually get, suddenly I thought of other disturbers of the peace.

Crows Remind me of Prophets

Crows raucous above me
seem to be crying with their caws,
"Why else have a voice
if not to disturb the peace?" 2/22/23

Disparagement springs not from a vacuum.

Thinking of Those Who Disparage

How can those who disparage
not nurse disparagement beneath their shell?
Too painful to remember
or too shameful, if remembered, to tell. 2/23/23

Raised Catholic, I spy Mary in other guises.

An Altar to Lono

There's a haven of refuge in Hawaii
honoring Lono, the goddess of forgiveness,
where anyone seeking sanctuary can find it.
Would that we each had an altar
to Lono in an inner grotto
(Catholics smile to have Mary)
where a candle is ever lit. 2/24/23

"Let your life speak" strikes to the core.

I Wonder if I Got it Backwards

That the scribe's back was to his Pharaoh—
eyes open but unfocused,
papyrus on lap and stylus in hand,
intently listening for what to write—
struck me wonderfully when in Egypt
to discover a brother across time.
But now I wonder if I got it backwards.
Perhaps with scroll in hand
it's Pharaoh (a.k.a. God) who is waiting
to record the next word my life speaks. 2/25/23

Waiting for distant drama misses the dramatic at hand.

Soft Revelations, are They not Endless?

Woodstove warming,
dog in lap sleeping,
dark sky brightening—
soft revelations.
Are they not endless
in the kingdom at hand? 2/25/23

I love when I expect a pleasant show, with a close friend in the cast, and am bowled over by two revelations.

You Could Hear a Pin Drop

Is there higher praise
for every player on the stage
when the audience is so rapt
watching twelve angry men
you could hear a pin drop?
It was as if each person viewing,
thanks to the magic wrought,
was transfixed by two revelations.
One was awe before the magnitude of the meaning
of a jury of quite distinct peers
deciding with due deliberation nothing less
than a human being's guilt or exoneration!
The second was more subliminal—
a recognition at some deep level
that each of the quite distinct viewers
was a composite of all twelve.
Don't take my word for it.
Go at next opportunity to *12 Angry Men.*
If it's as well performed
as the one I just had the privilege to see,
you'll be able to hear a pin drop. 2/27/23

Each next thing with love—
is there any other way
this side of heaven? 3/21/23

Isn't it as much what we leave behind as what we take with us?

Decidedly Making a Difference

Returning to Great Mystery
after making a decided difference
in the hearts of our friends—
wouldn't you say
we'd then have something amazing
to show for our being here,
for decidedly making a difference? 3/21/23

This will speak to those who understand you can have relationships with trees. To those who have not had the pleasure and privilege, just imagine.

I Like to Think the Trees Will Remember

The surrounding trees
were here before me,
will be here when I'm gone.
I like to think they'll remember as will I
our time together. 3/24/23

Think the odds against—
like winning the lottery
each friend in your life! 3/24/23

Acknowledge you've been indoctrinated if the pronoun gives you trouble.

Put a Face on God

Put a face on God.
Imagine her gazing with tenderness
on you who emerged clothed in light
from the warmth of her womb. 3/25/23

How call it an It
when incredibly it birthed
persons like yourself? 3/25/23

Imagine the drama in God's heart not to know our choices at each next fork in the road. But God knows all things, you protest. And miss, I respond, the drama?

God on the Edge of Her Seat

"That's my story and I'm sticking to it."
Isn't it magnificent
that we each *have* a story,
one (like that of the universe)
not yet finished?
Imagine God sitting on the edge of her seat
breathlessly waiting to read
the next page in each story,
pumping courage to us each. 3/26/23

A comforting prayer to start the day with.

May I Softly Lay My Head

May softly I lay my head
tonight upon my pillow
remembering acts of kindness or courage
I've tucked on this day
into the heart of the world. 3/26/23

Francis deluded
to call the Sun his brother?
Or are we not to? 3/26/23

I used to aim for the sunrise, now if I can make it up in time I aim for dawn.

What Human Pageantry Compares?

O the sky this morning!
Deep dark
then hint of gray
touch of rose
gathering of orange
spellbinding crimson
all inaugurating blue!
Decked out in such color
what human pageantry compares? 3/29/23

Just hanging with God—
what if it were that simple,
your reason to pray? 3/30/23

It's enough to sit
in the company of trees,
breathing together. 3/30/23

Don't knock fear for what it can motivate.

A Saving Fright

Does not each breathing
come from the blue mantle
wrapped around the shoulders
of the one we call Mother?
It's not a stretch
to say our breathing and hers
are one and the same.
Granted it's a fright
to realize our greedy actions
are fouling her blue mantle
but a saving fright really
if it wakes enough in time. 3/31/23

How not be struck dumb
to imagine we are sought,
not only seeking. 4/1/23

Dorothy and Theodore—it's in their very names.

God's Gift

We say it with mocking.
There he goes, God's gift to the world.
Who does she think she is, God's gift?
But are we not each
to the universe God's gift? 4/6/23

Whom might you forgive
in your heart of hearts today?
Bring fire from heaven. 4/12/23

Could it be if instead of a wild fluke, we've at root been intended?

Embodying the Universe's Heart

The universe has been growing a heart
for some fourteen billion years.
What greater dignity
than embodying it in your manner
of treating the next one you meet. 4/13/23

Americans enamored of their country's ideals will pause on April 15th to remember one of the wisest of their tribe departing.

Questions Lincoln Left Us

At 7:22 this morning
one hundred and fifty-eight years ago
the man wishing malice toward none and charity for all
took his last labored breath
leaving us to labor on.
Might there be someone
for whom you have been nurturing resentment,
or another who is excluded from the reach
of the healing of your forgiveness?
It is good for spirited Americans
(and any spirited across Earth)
to remember Abraham Lincoln. 4/15/23

Whatever science discovers or conjectures, take it deeper.

Black Holes Birthing Light

Black holes we are told swallow light,
but that never stopped the Big Bang
from flaring forth from the blackest.
Next time it feels you are in one
despairing light ever to return,
breathe deep and wait on the universe
to ignite in your heart a new flaring forth. 4/15/23

Do you really think you just happen to be here?

Reason to Get Up in the Morning

Would you not be astounded
to realize you're the tip of the vanguard
of a fourteen-billion-year thrust
toward the amorization of the cosmos?
Bosh, you say, I'm nothing
but a random fluke in the maelstrom.
Undeterred I counter,
imagine instead you've been intended
to bring to the jewel of the universe still birthing
an absolutely unique gift?
Can you think of a better reason
to get up in the morning? 4/16/23

Start with the one in the mirror when dealing out compassion.

Climbing Mt. Compassion

What if you were to discover
that the thing about yourself you like least
(or loathe the most)
when it comes to the climbing of Mt. Compassion
were in fact your greatest asset?
Accept yourself and you can accept anyone!
What mountaineer inspiring others to follow
might you then not become? 4/16/23

Not to knock the possibility of angels up there, but what of the ones down here who have rousingly cheered you on?

Bring Angels Down to Earth

What if angels are simply embedded presences—
rallying you, cheering you on—
of those who have loved you?
What cloud of witnesses to your shining—
calling to you to keep heart,
to remember your gift!
Why else in your life
has been all their loving? 4/16/23

Rather than ruing an interior struggle, in my better moments I just sit back and watch them go at it. Nothing helps like humor for perspective.

Imagine Having to Live with These Guys

Every time Moose wants to bellow
Mouse peeps stay low, don't risk it.
Imagine having to live with these guys! 4/17/23

Why wait to pluck the ripe fruit?

No Need to Wait till You're Eighty

You think I'm morbid
to think the garden I'm putting in
may given my years be my last?
Au contraire, it heightens the pleasure!
No need to wait till you're eighty.
If you're looking for revelation,
imagine this day of all yours on Earth
could be your final.
Horace's carpe diem
means pluck while it's here
today's ripe fruit. 4/17/23

Best kept secret of Friends—a meeting for discernment.

When at an Impasse

When at an impasse
yearning discernment about which way to go,
imagine having a small circle of friends
bent first on listening,
then offering thoughtful questions with no goal in mind
except to help you find clearness.
Something to think about
next time you're at an impasse. 4/18/23

Simply flip the switch
to full-hearted attention.
Feel the live current. 4/20/23

Poets help both to widen the lens and to sharpen the focus.

Next Time You Enter a Forest

You call them trees,
Cummings called them "leaping greenly spirits."
Next time you enter a forest
take Cummings with you. 4/21/23

Earth-prophet he's been called, following Teilhard.

Thank You, Thomas Berry

Collection of objects—
the way we've been conditioned
to think of the universe.
Communion of subjects—
settle into silence imagining it,
then rise shining.
Everywhere kin! 4/21/23

Just imagine them humming together.

All Humming with Sophia

Mary interlaced with Isis and Kwan Yin,
all humming with Sophia—
each morning fortification,
each evening comfort. 4/21/23

Crows clamor above—
distracting my reverie
or announcing God? 4/21/23

Just let it sink in.

Caught on Tape

You'd think it was Blacks they were talking about,
but this time it was reporters.
"O for the old days
when we could lynch 'em and bury 'em,
the dozers are ready."
Caught on tape four lost their jobs,
but how many others
in seats of power across the land
are too discreet to be caught on tape?
Not 1923 we're talking,
but 2023!
Lord have mercy. 4/23/23

Does sky not bend own
to kiss the amorous ground
upon which we stand? 4/23/23

Participating
in the vision quest of God—
talk about drama! 4/23/23

Who needs bolstering more?

The Choir Too Needs Preaching

Preaching to the choir would seem superfluous
for have not these seen the light?
But remember what comes after baptism.
When the going gets tough,
confirmation absolutely is needed
for the choir to keep singing. 4/25/23

Imagine the Welcome He's Receiving

"Anybody seen my old friend Abraham...
my old friend John...
my old friend Martin...
my old friend Bobby...
can you tell me where they've gone?"
So sang Harry Belafonte.
Imagine the welcoming he's receiving
from his old friends now. 4/26/23

Could things be more precarious?

Either Way a Storm is Coming

Unless convicted
(what a storm if he is)
he'll win the nomination,
lose the election,
and guaranteed will once again
scream bloody murder it was stolen
(what a storm then).
We'll see if democracy already teetering
can keep standing through the storm,
whichever one. 4/26/23

Gigantic sorrow
if when final breath expires
songs remain unsung. 4/26/23

This will speak to lovers of trees.

Cathedral Awe

The Hidden Life of Trees,
gift from a friend knowing me well.
I've just finished lingering my way through it
as one might on a hushed walk
in a forest awash with presence—
cathedral awe overhead, underfoot.
You are so beautiful to me,
sang Joe Cocker to his love,
sing I to the trees. 4/26/23

Isn't creativity at the core?

Go Easy on the Dogma

Go easy on the dogma—
there's too much creativity going on
to try nailing things down.
Trust only that the band
without your note would miss a beat. 4/27/23

Neither can you, I'm guessing, get over Buddha and Jesus.

Cool Hopeful Breeze

I can't get over Buddha and Jesus,
both depicted as raising a hand
gesturing "Fear not"
from hearts of compassion.
What furnaces of fire must they themselves
have passed through to get there?
For the rest of us still in the furnace,
what cool hopeful breeze of hope. 4/29/23

Something to ponder for a year.

Each Jewel Enhances the Light

Of course light enhances each jewel
(in the dark no sapphire fires)
but have you ever considered
that each jewel enhances the light?
Ponder that for a year
as you wonder why you're here. 4/30/23

Forgiveness seems weak
to the calculating mind—
mustn't one keep score? 5/7/23

Still Trying to Fathom It

Seventy-four years ago today
I made my First Holy Communion.
Some things you remember.
Supposedly we could fathom it then
having reach the proverbial age of reason,
but at 81 I'm still trying to fathom it,
the staggering holiness of communion. 5/8/23

Loren Eiseley hewed to the essence: "We are in a creative universe. Let us then create."

Even if Your Best is a Stammer

Had Shakespeare thrown up his hands
in futility before a blank page,
or Michelangelo before a block of marble,
or Van Gogh before an empty canvas,
think what awesome losses to the world.
Even if your best is a stammer,
the world will mourn not to hear it. 5/5/23

It's always tricky to speak in superlatives, but is it not sometimes called for?

Greatest Revelation of Our Age

Draw into your awareness
that whatever its form
your creativity this day will extend
the still birthing Creation!
Greatest revelation of our age?
Not cosmos but cosmogenesis! 5/6/23

"Supernatural"—
right there the problem began.
Earth desacralyzed. 5/11/23

Thinking of my brother's bafflement years ago, "How could you start out Catholic and end up Quaker?" what follows reminds me how in a fundamental way I never left.

Communion, from Start to Finish

As a kid we called it going to Communion,
now it's called receiving the Eucharist.
Some in the same spirit
find it sufficient to celebrate
the wonder of it together
in silence. 5/8/23

As Mary Oliver has been the subject of more than a few of these ruminations, it feels fitting to accord to her the final one.

"A fact: one picks it up and reads it, and puts it down, and there is an end to it. But an idea! That one may pick up, and reflect upon, and oppose, and expand, and so pass a delighted afternoon together." (*Blue Pastures*, 57)

Twilight Farewell

I am pleased, fellow spirit-journeyer,
to have spent with you restful afternoons
or tranquil early mornings.
Ah, the twilight times.

BIOGRAPHICAL INFORMATION

Charlie Finn lives with his wife Penny north of Roanoke in Fincastle, Virginia. Both are retired and enjoying their life in the country, which includes tending to woodpile and many gardens. Their love of traveling takes them to visits with their children April and Adam in Tennessee and Texas, as well as to enticing points beyond. While Finn retired in 2015 from a 40-year career in counseling, which followed seven years as a high school English and Humanities teacher, he has not retired from his lifelong love of writing. His published writings included the following:

Circle of Grace: In Praise of Months and Seasons (1995)

Natural Highs: An Invitation to Wonder (1999)

For the Mystically Inclined (2002)

Contemplatively Sweet: Slow-Down Poems to Ponder (2004)

Earthtalks: Conjectures on the Spirit Journey (2004)

The Elixir of Air: Unguessed Gifts of Addiction (2005)

Deep Joy, Steep Challenge: 365 Poems on Parenting (2005

Earth Brother Jesus: Musings Free of Dogma (2005)

Embraced It Will Serve You: Encounters with Death (2006)

If a Child, Why not a Cosmos? Lovesongs to Earth and Evolution (2006)

Fuel for War: Patriotic Entrancement (2006)

Earth Pleasures: Pets, Plants, Trees, and Rain (2007)

Ithaca is the Journey: A Personal Odyssey (2007)

Steppingstones to the Civil War: Slavery Integral to Each (2008)

Aging Liberal Nostalgic for Vision (2008)

Empathy is the Key: Toward a Civil War Healing (2009)

Gentle Warrior John Yungblut: Guide on the Mystic's Journey (2009)

Full Heart Singing: Letters and Poems to a Girlchild (2009)

The Mastery of the Thing!: Transcendence in Counseling and Sports (2010)

Crafting Soul into Words: A Poet Sings of the Journey (2010)

Please Hear What I'm Not Saying: A Poem's Reach around the World (2011)

Roots and Wings: Gifts from Parents (2012)

John Yungblut: Passing the Mystical Torch (Pendle Hill Pamphlet #417, 2012)

Building a Memory Cathedral: Wisdom Figures (2013)

Building a Memory Cathedral: Years, Decades, Months (2014)

O the Mind, Mind has Mountains: Searching for the Heart of Hopkins (2015)

Mandalas Serving Memory: New Ways to Celebrate Your Life (2016)

New Under the Sun: Fecund 2016 (2016)

Focusing on Just One Gift: One Hundred Selected Poems (2017)

Great Day in the Morning: One Hundred Selected Poems (2018)

Sixty to Sing Of: A Wealth of Guardians (2018)

Winter Offerings: Poetry and Prose Dancing (2019)

Mining for Gold: Climbing Mount Empathy and Reclaiming the Mystical (2020)

Witness to the Unvanquished Human Spirit: Poetry for a Troubled Time (2020)

Who's to Say Every Bush is Not Burning?: Poetry during the Pandemic (2021)

Blue Plums on a Mat of Leaves: Ponderings at Break of Day (2023)

Glimmerings and Stammerings: Twilight Ruminations (2024)

Information about many of Finn's works can be found on his website, www.poetrybycharlescfinn.com. Inscribed copies can be ordered through him at charles.c.finn@gmail.com.